1939-1945
WORLD WAR TWO

AUTORE

Aymeric Lopez, Born in Lyon in 1986, he graduated in mechanical engineering and has been working in the military shipbuilding sector since 2009. He has always been fascinated by history, first by antiquity and then by the wars of the 20th century. A model maker since the age of 15, he has developed a particular interest in Italian WWII vessels, which are little known in his home country of France. For this reason he has become an expert thanks to frequent study and collection of documents, visiting museums and Italian military structures until he created a specific website on the subject born to share his passion.

ACKNOWLEDGEMENTS

The author and publisher thank you for kind grants and/or photo credits: collezione J.M. Campesino, collezione Francisco Andreu, collezione Famiglia Dequal, Archivo Fundación Yagüe, collezione Adriano Mantelli, Archivio Aeronautica Militare, collezione famiglia Bolesani, collezione Branguli, Collezione Bruno Dalpiaz, collezione Bernardo Monti, collezione E. Leproni , collezione Prospero Nuvoli, collezione famiglia Anderle, collezione Franco Bargoni, collezione famiglia Comelli, collezione Nino Bortolini, collezione Fernando Pina Rubio, collezione A. de Toro, collezione Patrick Laureau , collezioni Sebastian Aguilar, Betanya e Salvador, Archivos Estatales spagnoli, Bibliothèque nationale de France, Archivio Storico Provinciale di Bolzano), Museo Caproni , Museo Storico Italiano della Guerra, Bundesarchiv. The rest of the images where not otherwise indicated are from the author's collection.

Titolo: **ITALIANS IN SPAIN 1936-1937** Code.: **WTW-035 EN** by Aymeric Lopez
ISBN code: 978-88-93278577 First edition May 2022
Text: English Nr. of images: 138. layout: 177,8x254mm Cover & Art Design: Luca S. Cristini

WITNESS TO WAR (SOLDIERSHOP) is a trademark of Luca Cristini Editore, via Orio, 35/4 - 24050 Zanica (BG) ITALY.

WITNESS TO WAR

ITALIANS IN SPAIN 1936-1937

PHOTOS & IMAGES FROM WORLD WARTIME ARCHIVES

AYMERIC LOPEZ

INDICE

▲ The revolt in Morocco on the front page of the newspaper *La Voz* of July 18, 1936. National Library of Spain.

INTRODUCTION

THE ORIGINS OF THE SPANISH CIVIL WAR

Although the complete genesis of the Spanish conflict is not the main object of study of this book, which focuses on Italian participation in the Civil War, it's good to start by tracing the chronology of events that led to the outbreak of the conflict in the Iberian Peninsula.

A COUNTRY IN DECLINE

In 1898, Spain was defeated in the brief war against the United States, the last conflict of a century that marked the end of Spain's colonial empire. As a result of the Treaty of Paris, the country lost Cuba, Guam, Puerto Rico and the Philippines. All that remained of its empire were a few African possessions, completed in 1912 by the protectorate of Morocco. Spanish elites suddenly realized that their country had become a secondary player on the international stage, while the rapid defeat of the United States was perceived as a profound humiliation by society as a whole.

Internally, the country was struggling with many socio-economic difficulties, the most important of them being the agrarian problem. In 1928, almost 75% of the land belonged to 5% of the owners, and about 90% of Spain's 4,500,000 peasants earned less than one peseta a day, barely a quarter of the average wage. Regional disparities in industrial development, limited primarily to Catalonia and the Basque Country, paved the way for nationalist claims in these regions.

Politically, Spain returned to constitutional monarchy after the 1874 coup d'état in the guise of the restoration of the Bourbons, following the brief experience of the first republic proclaimed in February 1873. This regime was based on a two-party system in which fictitious political alternation was agreed upon between the two dynastic parties (liberal-conservative and liberal-fusionist) and ensured through the use of electoral fraud. The institution of universal suffrage for men over the age of 25 in 1890 did not fundamentally change the functioning of the system. The deep centralization that accompanied the restoration only strengthened Catalan and Basque nationalism. The first labor movements gave rise to the PSOE, founded in 1879, and the UGT union in 1888.

With the accession to the throne of Alfonso XIII in 1902, Spain began a timid modernization under the control of the army. During World War I, the country remained neutral, which contributed to its marginalization in Europe. In 1917, a revolutionary strike broke out, leading to the declaration of a state of emergency. The severe flu epidemic of 1918 only exacerbated the situation, while the Russian Revolution influenced the trade unions, which maintained centers of revolt throughout the country until 1921. Subsequent governments, unable to restore the situation due to political divisions on all sides, quickly followed until Miguel Primo de Rivera's coup on September 13, 1923. Recognized by the king, Primo de Rivera's dictatorship was to bring order to the country's corruption. For this purpose, the constitution was suspended, municipal councils were dissolved, and political parties were banned. While the CNT and the PCE were repressed, the PSOE and the UGT were tolerated by the regime. The policy of major works in the fields of infrastructure, irrigation and hydroelectric power initially allowed the regime to enjoy great popularity. But support for the dictatorship was short-lived: the Catalan bourgeoisie was quickly disillusioned with the centralist policies of the government and the deterioration of working conditions alienated the PSOE and the UGT from Rivera's plans. The crisis of 1929 had devastating effects on the country's economy, and Alfonso XIII forced the dictator to resign and go into exile in January 1930.

THE SECOND REPUBLIC

As a result of the dictatorship, the monarchy was seriously challenged by the Pact of San Sebastian, signed by the majority of Spanish republican movements. The idea of abolishing the monarchy also caught on in the army, where attempts at rebellion were bloodily suppressed. In order to gauge public opinion, the king and his head of government, Admiral Juan Bautista Aznar-Cabañas, decided to hold municipal elections on April 12, 1931. On the morning of April 13, partial results from the big cities gave a large majority to the Republicans.

Out of 50 provincial capitals, 40 saw the victory of the Republican lists. When the first results were announced, enthusiastic crowds formed in the main cities of the country, while the king summoned his ministers to announce that he was ready to face the consequences of this failure. In the end, however, the royalist candidates represented 50.17% of the total thanks to their good results in rural areas, against 48.03% for the Republicans. But Alfonso XIII had made up his mind: considering that remaining in power could lead to serious unrest, he decided to go into exile on April 14, but without abdicating. At first he went to France, then, in 1934 he settled permanently in Rome.

The same day of the results the Second Republic was proclaimed, although the constitution did not provide for municipal elections to change the regime in force. The elections of the Cortes Constitucionales of June 28, 1931 gave a large majority to the parties of the Republican Left, with 38.4% of the vote and 173 seats out of 470. The Socialists, led by moderate leader Julián Besteiro, obtained 24.5% of the vote and 116 seats. The 27.8% of the votes collected by the center were scattered among several parties, while the 9.7% of the votes of the right-wing parties marked their undeniable defeat. A center-left government governed the young republic, led by Manuel Azaña, a member of the Republican Left, appointed by the president of the republic, Niceto Alcalá Zamora.

In June 1932, under pressure from the PSOE and the UGT, Council President Azaña cancelled 61 meetings of the Accion Popular, the right-wing republican party of José María Gil-Robles, and banned the publication of the right-wing newspaper El Debate for two months. In August 1932, General José Sanjurjo Sacanell, who had joined the republic, attempted to overthrow it in order to restore the monarchy. Informed of the plot, Azaña let it happen in order to have a pretext to republicanize the army.

On November 19, 1933, the general election in the Cortes was won by the right, which took advantage of the disunity of the left and the instructions of the anarchists to abstain. This was the first election in which Spanish women were allowed to vote. The CEDA, which brings together the parties of the Republican Right under the leadership of José María Gil-Robles, was in the lead with 24.3% of the vote and 115 seats out of 472. The right-wing parties together took 242 seats, the centrists 131 and the left 99. President of the Republic Niceto Alcalá Zamora was supposed to call the leading party leader to form the new government. But under pressure from the PSOE and the UGT, Zamora turned to Alejandro Lerroux, leader of the Radical Republican Party, to form a cabinet of government. But the latter could do nothing without the CEDA of Gil Robles, who agreed to support him for a few months, even though his party had no ministerial posts.

▲ King Alfonso XIII in hussar uniform. (Photo credits: J.M. Campesino collection)

This submission brought criticism to Gil-Robles from the monarchists but also from his own party, which led him to ask for three ministerial portfolios in October 1934, while renouncing any government function for himself. The entry of three CEDA ministers into the government led to an armed uprising planned by the anarchist and Marxist left, called the "October Revolution," which affected Asturias in particular. The movement was violently repressed by General Francisco Franco Bahamonde, and government policy became very reactionary. In May 1935, five members of CEDA entered the government, including Gil-Robles who became Minister of War. In both camps, extremism was on the rise.

In February 1934, the Spanish Phalange, a nationalist and syndicalist organization founded on October 29, 1933 by José Antonio Primo de Rivera, son of the former dictator, merged with Ramiro Ledesma Ramos' JONS to form the FE de las JONS. Although the party was initially opposed to any reprisals against its opponents, its attitude changed after the "October Revolution."

To revive the left after the November 1933 defeat, Azaña sought to form a popular front. But in addition to his Izquierda Republicana and Unión Republicana parties, Azaña was forced to approach the PSOE to form a broad leftist coalition. However, the latter had become strongly radicalized since the social democratic tendency led by Juliàn Besteiro had been removed from the leadership in 1932. After several months in prison following the violence of October 1934, Largo Caballero became the main leader of the PSOE. Nicknamed the Spanish Lenin, he imposed his revolutionary tendency on the party. Hardening his speech, Azaña succeeded in forming the Frente Popular, which included the PSOE and the PCE on October 20, 1935.

THE POPULAR FRONT TAKES OVER

In January 1936, with the country proving ungovernable, President Alcalá Zamora decided to dissolve the Cortes and call new elections. The campaign took place in a poisonous atmosphere. On the right, José-Antonio Primo de Rivera told his supporters that *"if the result of the poll is contrary, dangerously contrary, to the eternal destinies of Spain, the Phalange will relegate with all its might the record of the poll to the rank of contempt"*. On the left, Largo Caballero warned that *"in the event of a right-wing victory in the elections, we will necessarily have to resort to open civil war"*. The elections were set for February 16, 1936. So that the CNT and FAI would not repeat their order of abstention as in 1933, the Frente Popular promised to grant amnesty to all prisoners of the "October Revolution of 1934," among whom were many anarchists. On the other hand, the right was divided at the polls, with the National Front wanted by Gil-Robles struggling to rally beyond CEDA.

Although the results of the elections are not known precisely, the main trends are indisputable. It was a clear victory for the Frente Popular, but not a massive one, as its score did not reach 50%, within 2% of the total right-wing vote. Since the electoral law guaranteed a comfortable majority to the winning coalition, the left obtained 263 seats out of 473, against the 163 of the right-wing parties.

▲ Miguel Primo de Rivera, dictator from 1923 to 1930.

▲ Sanjurjo on trial with other officers who participated in the coup attempt.

▼ Alejandro Lerroux in the November 1933 elections.

▲ Franco and Gil-Robles, minister of war from May to December 1935.

▼ President Alcalá Zamora visiting an air base.

Within the Frente Popular, the balance of power was more favorable to the Republican left than to the Marxist left. The government formed by Azaña included only members of the Izquierda Republicana and Unión Republicana: Azaña did not want to include socialists in his cabinet, and Largo Caballero opposed PSOE participation in the new government, fearing that Indalecio Prieto (the PSOE's second) would form a social democratic alliance. The CEDA recognized the victory of the Frente Popular, and the leader of the Falange gave instructions that members of his party should not adopt a hostile attitude toward the new government.

As soon as it took office, Azaña's government decreed an amnesty for

▲ In Barcelona, the prisoners of the "October Revolution of 1934" were released on February 16, 1936.

prisoners of the 1934 "October Revolution" before embarking on agrarian reform and launching the reorganization of the military command, appointing generals close to the republic to key posts and removing from Madrid those deemed less loyal. In a difficult economic situation, the victory of the Frente Popular encouraged workers and peasants to make demands that went far beyond the capacity of the industrial and agricultural sectors, multiplying strikes and occupations. But the most serious problem for the government was the rise of extremism in the left wing of the Frente Popular, which it was unable to handle. The PSOE believed that the country was ripe for revolution. Largo Caballero, increasingly influenced by his advisor Álvarez del Vayo, a member of the Comintern, declared, "The revolution we want can only be achieved through violence." Militias were formed in all the leftist organizations, including the highly effective MAOC of the PCE led by Italian Ettore Vanni, a member of the Comintern.

On February 27, the offices of the Phalange were closed and the next day four Phalangist workers who were members of the CONS were killed. On March 4, two Phalangist students were found dead. The next day, the Phalangist press was banned, while on March 11, a Carlist student was assassinated in broad daylight in Madrid. The next day, four Phalangist students targeted PSOE parliamentarian Luis Jiménez de Asúa. Although he escaped the assassination attempt unscathed, his escort officer was not so lucky. The government reacted on March 14 by imprisoning José-Antonio Primo de Rivera and 2,000 Falangist leaders, which did not prevent the party from organizing an armed response.On April 3, 1936, Indalecio Prieto presented a motion to the Cortes to impeach the president of the republic, Alcalá Zamora, which was approved by 238 votes to 5. On May 10, Manuel Azaña replaced him as President of the Republic and appointed Galician Santiago Casares Quiroga as President of the Council. By-elections were held in May in constituencies deemed to be right-wing, following the annulment of the February votes by the Commission on the Proceedings of the Cortes, dominated by the Frente Popular. It should be noted that Prieto refused to chair the commission in protest of the irregularities it found. As a result of the terror caused by the left, the province of Granada, a right-wing stronghold, shifted to the left: of the 13 seats at stake, all were won by Frente Popular candidates, while the right won 7 seats in February and the center 3. These partial elections allowed the PSOE to become the first party in the Cortes with 99 seats. However, the party continued to refuse to enter the government, preferring to continue its revolutionary over-reach as the country sank into anarchy. The republican right began to disintegrate: the most fanatical massed in the outlawed Phalange.

As soon as the first unrest broke out, a part of the military began to plot. General Emilio Mola Vidal gathered some officers on March 8 to outline an embryonic revolt based on the EMU, while the leftist military gathered within the UMRA. The conspirators did not act discreetly and it is very likely that the government was informed. Nevertheless, the government preferred to let it happen, as in the case of the aborted Sanjurjo coup, thinking it could contain the movement and hoping to take advantage of the situation later.

On June 26, 1936, Franco, who had so far refused all offers from the conspirators, wrote a very ambiguous letter to Santiago Casares Quiroga, President of the Council, expressing the officers' concern about the disorder. Assassinations and punitive expeditions intensified on both sides. In the four months following the elections, no fewer than 269 people were killed and 1278 wounded. On the evening of July 12, a group from the Guardia de Asalto, a unit created by the Frente Popular to protect itself from a Guardia Civil deemed too right-wing, arrested monarchist leader José Calvo Sotelo. The next morning, his body was found in a ditch near Madrid. This assassination served as an electric shock: Franco rallied the conspirators. Military revolt broke out on July 17 in Morocco and on July 18 in mainland Spain: it was the beginning of the Civil War.

REASONS FOR THE ITALIAN INTERVENTION

The Spanish Civil War became an international interest very quickly. First, out of necessity, because both sides lacked weapons and equipment from the beginning and therefore turned abroad. Second, because the conflict was very ideologically marked and was to serve as a stage for the expression of all extremes of Europe, right and left.

▲ Niceto Alcalá Zamora (left), President of the Republic, and Manuel Azaña, President of the Council.

▲ General José Sanjurjo, instigator of the aborted coup of August 1932. (Photo credit: J.M. Campesino Collection)

In four days, between July 17 and 21, the Spanish armed forces were clearly divided between the two camps: while the air force and navy remained mostly loyal to the government, 24 out of 40 infantry regiments switched to the rebel camp. The Guardia de Asalto remained predominantly loyalist, with 11 out of 18 groups, while the Guardia Civil was divided between 108 loyalist and 109 rebel companies. The Tercio, the foreign legion, was largely on the rebels' side, as were the Moroccan regulars. The balance of power was clearly on the side of the Republicans. If the rebellion won easily in Morocco, the Canary Islands and the Balearic Islands (with the exception of Menorca), the situation was much more complicated on the continent, where most of the large cities remained loyal to the republic, including Madrid, Barcelona and Bilbao.

The government led by José Giral Pereira, who replaced Casares, reacted quickly by ordering the dissolution of the rebel units, arming the militias and training them for the future EPR. The leader of the insurrection, General Sanjurjo, died on July 20 in the crash of the plane that was to take him back from Portugal to Spain. Deprived of its leader and unable to occupy the main cities of the continent, the rebellion urgently needed to consolidate its positions, especially in Andalusia, by repatriating the military units in Morocco under the orders of General Franco, namely 30,000 men of the Tercio and regulars. But for this, the Nationalists needed outside help. They had only three Fokker F.VII b3m transports, the cargo ships Cabo Espartel and Ciudad de Algeciras, the destroyer Churruca (which passed to the Republican side after the first crossing between Ceuta and Cadiz following the revolt of the crews) and the gunboats Dato, Cánovas del Castillo and Lauria, the last two passed to the Nationalist side on July 18 when Cadiz was taken. The fleet, which remained primarily Loyalist, was ordered to sail to the Strait of Gibraltar to prevent the Nationalists from repatriating their troops to the mainland.

▲ Manuel Azaña and General Francisco Franco, who led the repression against the "October Revolution of 1934".

▲ José Antonio Primo de Rivera, founder of the Spanish Phalange.

On July 19, the same day Giral Pereira sent a telegram to France seeking Leon Blum's help, General Franco instructed Maj. Giuseppe Luccardi, stationed at the Italian consulate in Tangier, to ask the Italian government for the purchase of transport planes. The next day, Luccardi sent three telegrams to the SIM to inform them of Franco's request. The latter decided to give more weight to his request by sending on the evening of the 19th to Rome, via Portugal, the journalist Luis Bolìn of the monarchist newspaper *ABC*, so that Franco's request could be countersigned by Sanjurjo. Bolìn was received on the morning of July 22 by the foreign minister, Galeazzo Ciano. Hinting at a possible agreement on the sale, Ciano asked him to return the next day. But on July 23, Filippo Anfuso, Ciano's secretary, informed Bolìn that Italy could not accede to his request, officially for lack of available aircraft. Meanwhile, Mussolini had read Luccardi's telegrams and informed Ciano that he refused to help the insurgents. He considered the venture uncertain and feared exposing his country to open war immediately after the invasion of Ethiopia.

On July 22, General Mola gathered some representatives of the royalists and explained the difficulties of the insurrection. At the end of the meeting, the monarchists decided to send two delegations to Berlin and Rome to explain to the German and Italian governments the dangers of the Popular Front France helping the government in Madrid. The mission that arrived in Rome on the evening of July 24 was composed of Luìs Zeurunegui, Pedro San Rodríguez and Antonio Goicoechea, the monarchist leader in the Cortes. The latter had been received by Mussolini in March 1934 to seek support in arms and currency for a potential Carlist revolt. If the revolt did not take place, Italy had promised 1.5 million pesetas to the Carlists and had paid at least 500,000. When Ciano received the monarchist delegation on the morning of July 25, Italy's position toward the insurgents had changed. In fact, the Italian ambassador to France, Vittorio Cerruti, sent a coded telegram on the 23rd to inform the transalpine government that Léon Blum was ready to respond favorably to the Republican government's request for aid in arms and aircraft. The right-wing newspaper *L'Echo de Paris* had made the news on July 24, and the next day Ulrich von Hassell, the German ambassador in Rome, had informed Ciano of the French government's readiness to arm Madrid. Under these circumstances, Goicoechea had no difficulty in convincing Ciano to sell him 12 Savoia Marchetti S.81 on credit.

The 12 S.81s without nationality badges were assembled at Cagliari-Elmas airport between 28 and 29 July and left for Nador, in Spanish Morocco, on 30 July. Due to adverse winds that increased fuel consumption and insufficient preparation, only nine aircraft arrived at their destination: Dieci. Angelini's plane crashed into the sea. Mattalia's plane crashed in Algeria while Cpl. Ferrari's trimotor had to make an emergency landing in the French protectorate in Morocco, on the coast near the mouth of the Moulouya River, only 3 km from the border of the Spanish protectorate. Although the planes and pilots were disguised as civilians, their nationality was not in doubt for the French authorities and Italy's involvement in the Spanish conflict was made public the next day in the French press. From that moment on, there was no question of backing down, especially since Italy had also sent the cargo ship Morandi from La Spezia on July 27, loaded with ammunition, fuel and spare parts to support the air group.

Mussolini's choice to intervene on the side of the Spanish nationalists was therefore closely tied to France's attitude, even though in the end the first foreign aircraft to enter the conflict were Italian S.81s. He feared the lasting installation of a Popular Front regime in Spain, which would have the effect of strengthening the Paris-Madrid axis, while Italy was diplomatically isolated as a result of the sanctions decreed by the League of Nations in response to the invasion of Ethiopia.

▲ Popular demonstration at the announcement of the victory of the Frente Popular in the elections of February 16, 1936. (Photo credits: Archivos Estatales)

In addition, Franco promised Mussolini, through Luccardi, the establishment of a fascist republic and a clear diplomatic rapprochement in case of a nationalist victory, an argument not to be underestimated as Spain was a key country for Italian policy in the Mediterranean.

▲ General Emilio Mola Vidal, one of the main instigators of the July 1936 uprising, in the Burogs-Gamonal camp. (Photo credits: Archivo Fundación Yagüe)

▲ Fokker F.VII b/3m '20-4' before the July 1936 uprising. (Photo credits: Francisco Andreu collection on AviationCorner. net)

▲ The same aircraft in nationalist colors. It took part in the airlift over the Strait of Gibraltar.

▲ Moroccan regulars in Ceuta. (Photo credit: Archivo Fundación Yagüe)

▲ The S.81 of Cpl. Ferrari after its crash landing on the coast of the French protectorate in Morocco on July 30, 1936.

▲ Some of the crew commanded by Lt. Col. Ruggero Bonomi who flew the S.81 to Nador on July 30, 1936.

▶ The news of the Italian planes on the front page of *L'Humanité* of July 31, 1936. (Credits: Bibliothèque nationale de France)

1 - A GRADUAL ENTRY INTO THE SCENE

In the first months of the civil war and up until the battle of Madrid, the advance of the nationalist forces could lead one to believe that the conflict would end quickly. Italy tried to provide decisive support to the insurgents by sending increasing, though still limited, numbers of troops and equipment, both to keep pace with Germany and to counter French aid to the Republicans in order to gain influence in the western Mediterranean.

NATIONALISTS TAKE THE INITIATIVE

The day after the insurrection, the first emergency for the Nationalists was the transfer of all troops from Morocco to the metropolis. On August 5, 2,500 men and a battery of 105 mm cannons were able to cross the Strait of Gibraltar under the protection of the Dato and Uad Quert gunboats and the Italian S.81, which put the Republican destroyer Lepanto to flight.

The arrival of Moroccan troops in Andalusia allowed the conquest of Merida on August 8 and Badajoz between 13 and 14, ensuring the conjunction with the nationalist troops in the north and the control of most of the Portuguese border. Important successes were also obtained by the Nationalists in Andalusia, in particular the taking of Huelva and its mines and the connection with the city of Granada. In the Basque Country, the insurgents were also on the offensive: on September 4, Mola's forces took Irún, on the border with France, before capturing San Sebastian on September 15.

After the conjunction of the nationalist forces from the north and south, the offensive toward Madrid could begin. On September 3, the 5,000 men of Lieutenant Coronel Yagüe took Talavera de la Reina, in the Tagus Valley, a strategically important junction on the march to the capital. The next day, after Giral's resignation, a new republican government was formed: Largo Caballero became

▲ One of the first 12 Fiat CR.32 of the Aviación del Tercio that landed from the Nereide at Melilla on August 14, 1936. (Dequal family)

president of the council and minister of war, while Indalecio Prieto assumed the portfolios of navy and aviation. For the first time, communists entered the government. The new cabinet was urged to prepare for the defense of Madrid. On September 7, the Republicans counterattacked in an unsuccessful attempt to retake Talavera.On September 27, the lifting of the siege of the alcázar of Toledo, where José Moscardó Ituarte had been holding out since July 22 with 1,000 men, by the regulares of General José Enrique Varela had an enormous impact. In return, the Nationalists were several days behind and their main objective was Madrid, a strategic and political objective firmly held by the Republicans, despite the departure of the Caballero government for Valencia on November 7.

On September 29, 1936, the Nationalist naval victory in the Strait of Gibraltar, achieved with the commissioning of the cruisers Canarias and Almirante Cervera at the expense of the destroyers Gravina and Almirante Ferrándiz, greatly facilitated the transfer of units from Morocco and constituted a turning point in the balance of power between the navies of the two sides.

DOMESTIC AND INTERNATIONAL IMPLICATIONS OF THE ITALIAN INTERVENTION

Mussolini's decision to aid the Spanish insurgents was dictated primarily by rivalry with France, jealousy of Germany, and national and personal prestige. The strategic and economic aspects took second place, even if the Duce was well aware of the advantages that a nationalist victory could bring him and the dangers that a Popular Front government in Spain would have represented.

Italy emerged victorious from the war in Ethiopia and Mussolini was convinced that the Spanish adventure would be short and inexpensive compared to the strategic advantages that he could get from the establishment of a friendly regime in the Iberian Peninsula. Despite the victory, the colonial war had swallowed up important resources and forced the postponement of programs to modernize the armed forces. In this rather unfavorable context, Mussolini did not bother to consult or inform his chief of general staff, Marshal Pietro Badoglio, of his decision to intervene in Spain. More than budgetary issues, the SMRE feared a deterioration of relations with France and England, at a time when Italy's relations with the SoN were beginning to improve.

▲ The Republican torpedo boat Lepanto at Port Mahon in 1935.

General Federico Baistrocchi, Undersecretary of State for War and Chief of the Army Staff, the only high-ranking officer to openly express his reservations about the policy of intervention in Spain, was dismissed on October 7, 1936 and replaced by General Alberto Pariani. Although initially Pariani was no more convinced than his predecessor of the merits of the enterprise, his good relations with the Minister of Foreign Affairs, Galeazzo Ciano, allowed him to adhere to Mussolini's position.

On September 4, 1936, the "S" section was created within the SIM with the aim of managing all aspects related to the Italian intervention in Spain. Faced with the reluctance of the Air Force and Navy, Mussolini entrusted the coordination of operations to the Ministry of Foreign Affairs. Since Ciano had no expertise in the military field, he relied on General Mario Roatta, head of the SIM. The latter ensured the link with the SMRE, keeping it informed of all decisions and asking for advice and opinions. The initiative of an Italian-German rapprochement on the intervention in Spain was taken by Berlin, which sent Admiral Wilhelm Canaris to Rome to meet Roatta on August 4. However, it was not until August 26 that an agreement was signed between the two sides. It provided for the sending of two missions of military advisers, one Italian called MMIS and the other German, to the Nationalists. In the meeting between Roatta and Canaris on August 28, Italy and Germany formally agreed to renounce any territorial compensation in exchange for their aid to the Nationalists.

The meeting between Ciano and Hitler in Berchtesgaden on October 24, 1936 led to an increase in aid given by both countries to Franco. It was also an opportunity for the German leader to propose an ideological alliance with Rome. However, Mussolini wanted to continue to play on both sides of the fence: on the one hand, he did not want to be outdone by Germany in terms of the influence Italy wanted to exert in Spain; on the other hand, he wanted Britain to recognize the Italian empire in Ethiopia.

On November 18, 1936, Italy and Germany recognized the Gobierno del Estado Español, led by General Franco, as the only legitimate government in Spain.

▲ Nationalist troops marching in Irún after taking the city on September 5, 1936.

▲ Militiamen surrendering their weapons to French gendarmes to cross the border at Irún between September 4 and 5, 1936.

▲ Militiamen entrenched behind a barricade in San Sebastian in July 1936.

▼ Moroccan horsemen of the Tercio of Melilla preparing to cross the Strait of Gibraltar.

▲ General Mario Roatta, commander of the MMIS.

THE ACTIVITY OF THE ITALIAN MILITARY MISSION IN SPAIN

Arriving in Spain, the two military missions commanded by Roatta and Warlimont met successively with Queipo de Llano in Seville and Franco in Càceres. Their activities began on September 6. On October 5, the MMIS followed Franco's headquarters to Salamanca. MMIS communications passed through Tangier before being forwarded to SIM, which in turn forwarded them to the Ministry of Foreign Affairs and the various commands involved. For communications addressed to Italy, Roatta took the pseudonym of Colli, and that of Mancini for those exchanged within the MMIS or to the Spanish.

Even before the arrival of the MMIS, Franco requested, on September 3, through Major Luccardi, to send 24 combat aircraft. With the activation of the MMIS, Franco's requests multiplied and concerned the supply of naval equipment to complete the ships under construction, torpedo boats and submarines. Unable to transfer all of these materials without the knowledge of agents of other powers, Rome refused delivery of some of them on September 22. Roatta went to the various fronts to inform Rome of the military situation throughout the peninsula, drawing a precise picture of the organization and tactics of the Nationalists, their weaknesses and strengths, portraits of their leaders and their relationships, the sharp differences between the Phalangists and the Royalists, and giving his feelings about the attitude of the population toward the insurgents in the territories under their control. After a brief passage to Morocco, Roatta returned to Rome on September 22 to report the situation to Ciano and the various staffs. He expressed his confidence in the Nationalists' chances of victory, due to the Republicans' moral and organizational inferiority, and encouraged Rome to continue and strengthen its involvement with the Nationalists.

▲ Left: Cpl. Vincenzo Dequal, aka Paride Limonesi, in the uniform of the Tercio. (Photo credit: Dequal family)
Right: Col. Ruggero Bonomi, commander of the Tercio Aviación.

▲ Moroccan legionnaires attending the landing of the Fiat CR.32 in Melilla on August 14, 1936. (Photo credits: Aeronautica Militare)

▼ Personnel of the XVI Gr.C. aboard the Nereide in La Spezia on August 7, 1936. (Photo credit: Dequal family)

▲ S.81 at the airport of Nador on August 4, 1936. (Photo credits: E. Leproni collection)

▼ The Nereide in Melilla on August 14, 1936. (Photo credits: Dequal family)

Upon his return to Spain on October 16, Roatta was summoned by Franco, who informed him that fifteen Soviet cargo ships loaded with arms and ammunition had docked in Cartagena. As a result, Franco asked Italy and Germany to increase their material aid in what he called a "crusade against Bolshevism." The new situation created by the USSR's massive aid to the Republicans forced both Italy and Germany to reconsider their general policy of support for the Nationalists as they tried to put on a good face within the non-intervention committee...

BIRTH OF THE TERCIO AVIATION

The cargo ship Morandi, which left La Spezia on July 27th, as mentioned in the previous article, docked in Melilla on August 3rd at 9:30 a.m. with the necessary equipment to support the group of 9 S.81 aircraft that had arrived on July 30th and had been idle for lack of fuel. The three-engine planes were then able to begin their surveillance of the Strait of Gibraltar to facilitate the transit of nationalist troops. To limit international protests, the S.81s were transferred to an ad hoc unit of the Tercio de Extranjeros created on July 31, commanded by Col. Ruggero Bonomi (alias Francesco Federigi) and called Aviación del Tercio. Although the crews were Italian, they wore the uniforms of the legion. On August 4, the 8 operational S.81s were transferred from Nador to Tetouan, Franco's headquarters, where they were welcomed by General Alfredo Kindelán y Duany, commander in chief of the Nationalist Air Force.

The same day, 2 S.81 attacked the destroyer Almirante Valdès, forcing it to suspend the bombardment of Larache. On the morning of August 7, 3 S.81 carried out their first mission over Spain, bombing the Republican Breguet XIX stationed at Guadix in the Sierra Nevada. On the same day, Erasi's tri-motor attacked unsuccessfully the cruiser Libertad in the Strait of Gibraltar. On August 9, 6 S.81 were reassigned to the Seville-Tablada airfield to more effectively support Franco's troops. However, they had to return to Tetouan on August 12 because all logistics were still there.

▼ Fiat CR.32 at Tablada in September 1936. It bears the inscription "Monico Presente" on the fuselage, in memory of the pilot shot by the Republicans. (Photo credits: Dequal family)

▲ CR.32 of Cpl. Dequal after an emergency landing near Portalegre, Portugal, on August 31, 1936. (Dequal family)

▼ Portuguese authorities, Franco's allies, allow the recovery of Dequal's CR.32 on Sept. 3, 1936. (Photo credits: Dequal family)

▲ Fiat CR.32 just reassembled at Nador in August 1936. Note the painted roundel on the underside of the upper wing.

▼ Pilots and mechanics aboard the Aniene, which arrived in Vigo on August 27, 1936. (Photo credits: Adriano Mantelli collection)

▲ Pilots of the 2nd escuadrilla at Talavera de la Reina at the end of September 1936. (Photo credit: Adriano Mantelli collection)

▼ Left: SSgt. Guido Presel in front of his CR.32 at Tablada in September 1936. (Photo credits: Dequal family). Right: Maj. Fagnani (left) and Col. Bonomi at Tablada in October 1936. (Photo credits: Dequal family)

▲ S.81 heavily damaged upon landing at Talavera de la Reina on October 18, 1936. (Photo credits: Dequal family)

▼ Pilots of the 2nd escuadrilla reloading their fighter's refueling strips, due to the lack of machine gunners, at Talavera airfield in late September 1936. (Photo credits: Air Force)

During the night between 7 and 8 August, a second merchant ship, the Nereide (former Spanish coal ship Alicantino), dropped anchor in La Spezia with 12 CR.32 of the XVI Gr.C partially disassembled, under the command of cpl. Vincenzo Dequal. Pilots and mechanics, all volunteers, traveled under false identities. After a stopover in Cagliari, the ship docked in Melilla on August 14, where the staff was welcomed by the Italian consul. The decision to send CR.32 fighters to the Nationalists was made after the Italian authorities were informed of the delivery of Dewoitine D.372 and Potez 540 from Paris to the government in Madrid, the first plane landing at Prat de Llobregat on 7 August.

The CR.32, nicknamed "Chirri" (grasshoppers) by the Spanish, were reassembled in Nador and painted with the colors of the Nationalist Air Force: black circles on the sides of the fuselage (introduced by General Mola on 27 July), a black St Andrew's cross on the rudder (introduced on 8 August by Franco) and black stripes under the wings. Note that the lower part of the upper wing was originally decorated with Spanish tricolor roundels (red-yellow-indigo), probably for identification by international naval forces patrolling the Strait of Gibraltar. The 12 aircraft formed the 1st escuadrilla de caza del Tercio. On August 17, the first CR.32 to be reassembled made a test flight piloted by s.Lt. Ceccherelli, who achieved the first Italian air victory in the Spanish Civil War on the evening of 21 August at the expense of Captain Antonio Martin-Luna Lesundi's Nieuport Ni.52 C1, which was escorting the Potez 540 in a raid over Cordoba. Meanwhile, the squadron began its transfer to mainland Spain, to the Seville-Tablada airfield, where 3 CR.32s landed on August 18. On August 21, the Aviación del Tercio had 8 S.81 and 7 CR.32 at Tablada, while one S.81 was waiting for a replacement engine at Melilla and 5 CR.32 were being assembled at Tetouan. On August 22, 2 S.81 bombed the CAMPSA fuel depots in Malaga: the fire lasted several days. On August 24, an S.81 was destroyed by a bomb explosion during loading on board, killing 3 armor personnel. The last CR.32 of the 1.a escuadrilla arrived in Tablada on August 27. On the same day, Fiat CR.32s faced Dewoitine D.372s for the first time over Guadix, shooting down that of Lieutenant Antonio de Haro López. The Italian planes were incessantly active, either in ground support for the Nationalist troops, attacking strategic targets in Republican territory, seeking air superiority or attacking enemy ships. During the night between August 27 and 28, the S.81 piloted by Ettore Muti damaged the cruiser Cervantes at anchor in Malága.

▲ Lt. Ceccherelli landing on a mule at Talavera de la Reina in October 1936. (Photo credits: Dequal family)

On August 10, the commercial ship Aniene departed from La Spezia with 9 Fiat CR.32 on board, commanded by Lieutenant Dante Olivero. While the former boat Ebro, which had just passed under the Italian flag, was calling at Cagliari, the Italians decided to replace its Spanish crew for fear that they would divert the ship to a Republican port. Stranded for a week in Cagliari, the Aniene did not arrive in Vigo, Galicia, until August 27 with her cargo of 9 CR.32s. Aircraft and personnel were transferred by train to Seville to be deployed on the field of Tablada on August 30 to form the 2nd escuadrilla de caza del Tercio.

On the same 27 August, 3 CR.32 under the command of Lt. Monico were transferred to Cáceres, Extremadura. On August 31, CR.32 piloted by Lt. Monico and Sgt. Castellani were shot down over Oropesa, not far from Madrid, in a fight with 3 Dewoitine D.372, a Hawker Furry and some Nieuport Ni.52 of the escuadrilla España (also called escuadrilla Malraux) based in Talavera de la Reina. While Castellani managed to make an emergency landing in no man's land near Villanueva de la Serena and managed to reach the Nationalist lines on foot, Monico was captured by the Republicans and shot. He was the first Italian pilot to die in this war. The Italian formation should have been completed by 3 CR.32 led by Cpl. Dequal, but they were forced to make a crash landing towards Portalegre, Portugal, due to a navigational error caused by a compass failure while en route to Cáceres. After this episode, Bonomi ordered them to fly in a formation of at least six aircraft.

On September 9, in order to support the Nationalist troops defending Talavera de la Reina, 9 CR.32 of the 1st escuadrilla Dequal and 3 S.81 were sent to Caceres. On September 11, in the space of three sorties, the CR.32s shot down seven Republican planes: one Dewoitine 372, two Breguet XIX and four Ni.52. This episode would be at the origin of the nickname "Cucaracha" (cockroach in Spanish) given to Dequal's fighter group and of the emblem adopted since April 1937 by the Italian fighters in Spain, which represents a cockroach wearing a red fez and playing a saxophone from which a Republican aircraft emerges. The combat was followed from the ground by Moroccan legionaries who, enthusiastic about the skill of the Italian pilots, compared their mounts to the agile insect. Another explanation is the popularity of the Mexican revolutionary song in Italy, especially thanks to the film "Viva Villa" presented at the Venice Film Festival in 1934. On September 6, the future Spanish ace Joaquin Garcia Morato Castaño joined the Aviación del Tercio, followed on the 11th by Captain Ángel Salas Larrazábal and on the 15th by Lieutenant Julio Salvador Díaz Benjumea. Despite the victories over the Republicans, whose level of training of mercenary pilots was much more disparate, the number of Fiat fighters decreased due to losses in combat, accidents and navigation errors. On September 17, 9 CR.32 remained in Càceres and 6 in Tablada, of which only a few were operational.

On September 24, Italian aircraft fighters were stationed at the Prado del Arca airfield (Talavera de la Reina) to provide more effective cover for the Nationalist offensive to lift the siege on the alcázar of Toledo. On September 25, CR.32s shot down two Ni.52s, a Loire 46, a Breguet XIX and a Potez 540, while the Nationalist air force lost a Junkers 52. On September 27, the Fiat escorted the S.81s that had gone to bomb Republican artillery positions around Toledo. With the loss of two Breguet XIX, a Potez 540 and a Dewoitine 372 between September 27 and 28, the Republican air force was forced to suspend almost all activity for fifteen days in the Madrid sector.

However, the Republican attack on Oviedo, Asturias, forced the Nationalists to delay their march on Madrid. Between October 16 and 17, 3 CR.32 and 3 S.81 were sent into the province of León. In two days, the S.81s destroyed seven planes in the airfield of Guajon and supported the Nationalist columns that succeeded in lifting the siege of Oviedo on September 17. On October 12, the cargo ship City of Messina, coming from La Spezia, docked in Cadiz where it disembarked 12 CR.32s. Once reassembled, the new fighters were incorporated into the two existing squadrons and sent in two waves of 6 to Talavera de la Reina on 18 and 21 October. Cpl. Carlo Albero Maccagno formally

▲ Potez 540 "Aquí te espero" shot down by capitán Ángel Salas and serg.magg. Gianlino Baschirotto on September 25, 1936.

took command of the 2nd escuadrilla de caza. At the same time, 21 IMAM Ro.37 reconnaissance bi-planes arrived in Spain: 10 were landed from the Aniene in Vigo on September 30 and 11 in Seville on October 20. Six Ro.37s were handed over to the Nationalist Air Force, while the others formed the 1st and 2nd OA squadrons under the command of Cpl. Raffaello Colacicchi and Sforza. The 1st sq.OA began to operate from the airfield of Talavera in mid-October.

On October 21, Maj. Tarciso Fagnani arrived in Talavera to replace Dequal as commander of the combat units. On November 3, he ordered the redeployment of the 14 operational CR.32s to the Torrijos airfield, which was much more discreet than Talavera and was the object of frequent Republican air attacks, including one carried out by 4 Soviet Tupolev SB-2 bombers on October 28 in what was their first mission on Iberian soil. The arrival of the Russian planes and their well-trained pilots changed the balance of power between the Republicans and the Nationalists.

▲ General José Millan Astray, commander of the Tercio, meets with Col. Bonomi and Cpl. Dequal in Càceres on September 24, 1936. (Photo credits: Dequal family)

ARRIVAL OF THE FIRST ITALIAN LAND UNITS

Transported together with Lieutenant Dante Olivero's CR.32 aboard the banana boat Aniene, the first 5 Italian L3 tanks landed in Vigo on August 27, 1936. Sent to Valladolid with the Italian training personnel, they formed a platoon under the command of Lieutenant Julio Tomariz Martel Sabra. After a month of training, they were employed on the Guipuzcoa front, where between September 13 and 15 they participated in the occupation of San Sebastian with General Mola's troops. On September 29, in Vigo, the steamer City of Benghazi landed another 10 L3 tanks, including 3 flamethrowers, 38 65/17 guns, 15 officers, 149 non-commissioned officers and soldiers, 4 trucks, 4 radio sets and a car. Incorporated into the Tercio, these forces gave birth to the rgpt. Italo-Spanish on a company of 15 L tanks, 7 batteries of 65/17 on 4-6 guns each, divided into 2 groups, 3 anti-tank sections of 65/17 on 2 guns each and a radio platoon.

On October 18, this mixed unit was reviewed by Franco and General Roatta before being sent to the Torrijos-Talavera sector, with the exception of the 7th and 8th btr. which went to the Ávila area. During the march to Madrid, the mixed troops were assigned to the Yagüe grouping, on the left wing of José Enrique Varela's force. At dawn on October 21, the I and II gr. of 65/17 participated in the preparation of the artillery, firing the first Italian grenades of the Civil War. The L3 tank company attacked Republican units in the Valmojado sector and then advanced on Navalcarnero, 30 km southwest of Madrid, where several hundred Republican soldiers were taken prisoner. On October 24, Colonel Monasterio Ituarte's cavalry column, supported by the agrupación carros-artilleria (i.e., the L 3 company and a group of 65/17), took the villages of Borox and Esquivias, then Seseña on October 25, cutting the Madrid-Aranjuez road. On the morning of the 29th, the Republicans counterattacked with the support of a company of 15 Soviet T-26 armored vehicles commanded by Mayor Paul Matisovitch Arman. At first they managed to penetrate Seseña before having to retreat under the fire of the 65/17 guns of the I Gr. The Nationalists lost an L3 while the Republicans left 3 tanks on the ground, 2 of which were recovered the following night.

▲ The first L3s to arrive in Spain traveling along Calle Loyola in San Sebastian in September 1936.

▲ The steamer City of Benghazi, which landed the Italian contingent at Vigo on September 29, 1936.

▼ Rodolfo Olivieri posing on his CV 35 at Navalcarnero in October 1936.

The Nationalist advance resumed on October 31. The Carros-Artillery group, assigned to the Asensio column, took Parla. On November 1, transferred to the Barrón column, the group reached Fuenlabrada, which was the object of a Republican counterattack on the 3rd, repulsed with the support of the guns of the I Gr.

The mixed Italian-Spanish units participated in the first battle of Madrid from November 7 to 9 and then in the second from November 15 onwards against the university campus, in which the company of L 3 was the first Nationalist unit to penetrate. On November 26, the training phase of the mixed units being considered over, the Italian personnel were withdrawn, leaving the equipment to the Spanish. The third offensive against Madrid, from November 29 to December 15, was another failure for the Nationalists.

▲ Effects of a Nationalist bombardment on the Puerta del Sol, Madrid, November 1936.

▲ Group of militiamen waiting to leave for Majorca in Port Mahon in August 1936. (Photo credits: Branguli collection on abc.es)

THE CASE OF THE BALEARIC ISLANDS

In the Balearic Islands, the July 18, 1936 revolt was successful in Mallorca and Ibiza, while Menorca remained loyal to the government. As a strategic point for the control of traffic in the western Mediterranean and between France and Africa, the Balearic Islands were an important element for Italian policy in the region.However, the game was not yet over, because, with control of Menorca, the Republican forces had a naval air base, while the insurgents could not expect any support from the mainland because the Republicans had an advantage at sea and in the air. From July 23, the Aeronáutica Naval, whose majority remained loyal to the government, bombed the Nationalist-controlled islands from Catalonia and Menorca with 11 Savoia S.62s, 4 Dornier Wals and the few operational Macchi M.18s.

Knowing they could not withstand a landing by Loyalist forces, Majorca's insurgents asked Italy for help. On August 2, Juan Thomas and Martin Pon Rodelló left the island on a German ship bound for Rome. Although their first attempts were unsuccessful, things changed after Italy obtained unofficial British consent to send military aid to the Balearic Islands, the Italian ambassador in London, Dino Grandi, having convinced the influential Winston Churchill that Rome had no territorial claims on the archipelago. Thus, Thomas and Pon were able to reach an agreement on August 13 for the purchase of 3 Savoia S.55 seaplanes, 3 Fiat CR.32 fighters, 3 20mm anti-aircraft batteries and ammunition. Meanwhile, two Republican naval formations sailed from Valencia and Barcelona on August 7. They carried an expeditionary force of 2,000 men for the former and 6,000 for the latter, commanded respectively by Guardia Civil Captain Manuel Ulibarri and Captain Alberto Bayo Giroud. The formation left from Valencia occupied the island of Formentera on August 8 and Ibiza on August 9, while Bayo's 6,000 men landed between Cuevas del Drach and Porto Cristo, on the

▲ The battleship Jaime I in Tenerife on May 5, 1936. She supports the Republican landing in Mallorca in August.

eastern coast of Majorca, on August 16, after a stop at Port Mahon to prepare the assault. They were supported by Aeronáutica Naval aircraft, the battleship Jaime I, the cruiser Libertad, the destroyers Almirante Miranda and Almirante Antequera, the submarines B-2, B-3 and B-4 and support ships. Soon the Republicans occupied a bridgehead 30 km wide and 5 km deep.

The insurgents needed immediate support to hold Majorca. As soon as they arrived on the island on August 19, the 3 S.55 X of the 31st St. commanded by Lieutenant Petrali and coming from Orbetello via Cagliari bombed the Republican bridgehead and the support ships, damaging two of them. On August 21, seven S.62s of the Republican air force from Port Mahon (Menorca) damaged Petrali's S.55 while it was at anchor in the bay of Palma. In order to avoid the same fate, the other two S.55, by then devoid of ammunition, returned to Orbetello on August 26, while repairs on the third aircraft were completed on September 9.

After a pause due to the action of the S.55, the Republicans resumed their advance on August 23 before stopping on the 26th to reorganize, when they were almost ready to break through the Nationalist lines. The island's military governor, Coronel Díaz de Freijó, did not believe in his 5,000 men's chances of resistance and wanted to negotiate with the Republicans. But the local leader of the Phalange, Alfonso de Zayas y de Bobadilla, who wanted to believe in the insurgents' success, asked Sainz Rodriguez to send an Italian military advisor. This request was supported on August 24 by C.F. Carlo Margottini, commander of the destroyer Malocello, which had arrived in Palma de Mallorca on August 16 to relieve the Mistral. Officially, the presence of the transalpine ships was justified by the protection of Italian citizens on the island. On the evening of August 19, the Italian naval force was completed by the arrival of the cruiser Fiume.

Mussolini, aware of the strategic importance of the archipelago for Italy, and at the same time anxious not to offend Franco, chose to send the squadron leader Arconovaldo Bonacorsi, a member of the MVSN, rather than an army officer. Bonacorsi, nicknamed Conde Rossi by the Spanish, arrived in Majorca on August 26, 1936 aboard a Cant Z.506, accompanied by Mag. Leone Gallo, who took command of the air force. After a meeting with Zayas, Bonacorsi formed a unit of volunteers called "Los Dragones de la Muerte" and led raids against the Republican bridgehead at Porto Cristo and San Severa. On the evening of August 27, the damaged cargo ship Emilio Morandi docked in Palma de Mallorca. It had on board 3 Fiat CR.32, 3 Macchi M.41 bis, 300 men and 12 Breda 20/65

▲ The S.55 X of Lt. Petrali in repair in Mallorca.

▲ Arconovaldo Bonacorsi, the MVSN member chosen by Mussolini to be military advisor in Mallorca.

▼ The Macchi M.41 just assembled on the dock of the port of Palma de Mallorca at the end of August 1936. The nationalist insignia has not yet been affixed to the fuselage and fin (Photo credits: Aymeric Lopez collection).

cannons. Disembarked during the night, the fighters were transported to the Son San Juan airfield located 8 km from the port and the first one was reassembled in a few hours. On August 28th at 12:30 p.m., Sergeant Guido Carestiato took off with the CR.32, which had been raised during the night, to strafe the Republican troops and the 6 S.62 anchored in Cala Morlanda. He damaged four of them before shooting down a fifth near Punta Amer, while an hour later, Cpl. De Agostinis, aboard the same CR.32, attacked 2 S.62 just after their take off in the bay of Porto Cristo. One of them managed to escape while the other was forced to make a crash landing. All aircraft landed from the Morandi were operational after two days and from then on carried out a series of missions against the Republican beachhead and naval targets.

On August 30, 3 Savoia S.81 commanded by Lt. Palazzolo were deployed to Palma de Mallorca to carry out raids against Minorca and the Catalan coast. On the evening of September 1, the three engines damaged the liner Marqués de Comillas which had to be towed to Port Mahon. The next day, the city of Cadiz was hit off Punta Amer. On September 3, an M.41 and an S.81 attacked the submarine B-3 that had been stationed for several days in front of Majorca to inform the Republicans of the movements of the Nationalist troops. Although damaged, the submarine managed to dive to avoid the attack.

During the night of September 3 to 4, Alberto Bayo began to withdraw his troops from the bridgehead, which was covered by artillery from the Jaime I and Libertad. Although Bonacorsi could have claimed credit for the Republican retreat, it was largely due to the activity of the Italian air force and the Republican government's impatience with the lack of results in Mallorca, when it needed reinforcements to counter the Nationalist offensive in the Tagus Valley. The Republicans evacuated Cabrera on September 12, Ibiza on the 14th and Formentera.

The retreat of the Republicans forced Ciano to abandon his desire to interfere in the political affairs of Majorca and to give up the occupation of Menorca, for fear of London's reaction. Bonacorsi was forced to return to Rome in December 1936, leaving Mallorca with a bad image of itself for being complicit in the repressive acts of the Phalange. More than 1,000 opponents were put to death without trial, or after a bogus trial. Rome, aware of these actions, allowed this to happen.

▲ Personnel and mascot of the Balearic fighter unit in front of the CR.32 at Son San Juan in September 1936 (Photo credits: Air Force)

▲ Republican S.62s machine-gunned by Fiat CR.32s and beached at Porto Cristo (Photo credits: Aymeric Lopez collection)

▼ Sgt. Guido Carestiato in front of a CR.32 at Son San Juan airfield in late August and early September 1936. The bat painted on the fuselage comes from the coat of arms of Palma de Mallorca.

▲ Italian personnel posing in front of a Breda 20/65 cannon in the port of Palma de Mallorca (Photo: Aymeric Lopez).

▼ Savoia S.81 in flight over Mallorca in September 1936. (Photo credit: Aeronautica Militare)

II – INCREASE EXTERNAL HELP

After the formation of the international brigades and the direct intervention of the USSR in the conflict alongside the republic, Italian support for the nationalists intensified in the air, on land, and at sea.

SOVIET ENTRY AND GREATER ITALIAN INVOLVEMENT

At the time of the July 1936 uprising, the USSR adopted a very cautious stance, as Stalin feared that Russian intervention would ruin his efforts to forge closer ties with France and England to curb German imperialism. He initially let the Comintern handle humanitarian aid to the Republicans, merely gathering information to assess the situation. Trotsky, then in exile, accused Stalin of having betrayed the Spanish Revolution. After the visit of a delegation of the ECP to Moscow at the end of August, the master of the Kremlin decided to actively intervene in the Spanish conflict, aware that by remaining on the sidelines, the USSR would lose credibility with foreign communist parties.

On August 21, 1936, Marcel Rosenberg, former deputy secretary of the SoN, was sent to Madrid as Soviet ambassador. He was accompanied by many Red Army officers, including General Ian Karlovich Berzin, former chief of intelligence, Vladimir E. Goriev, military attaché, Nikolai Kuznetsov, naval attaché, and Yakov Smushkevich as air force adviser. Mikhail Koltsov, a well-known Pravda correspondent, and filmmakers Roman Karmen and Boris Makadeyev were sent to the area to publicize the conflict in the USSR. As a result of the information provided by the NKVD about the critical situation in the republic, the Soviet military authorities prepare an emergency aid plan called Operation X, which is completed on September 14. On September 13, Juan Negrín, finance minister

▲ Arrival of Italian Legionnaires in Cadiz aboard the liner Lombardia on January 1, 1937. (Collection Bruno Dalpiaz)

▲ Largo Caballero speaks to militiamen in the Sierra de Guadarrama. His visits to this front earned him great popularity and helped him become president of the Council on September 4, 1936. (Photo credit: Archivos Estatales)

▼ The Soviet cargo ship Kursk arrives in the port of Alicante on November 3, 1936.

of the Spanish government led by Largo Caballero since September 4, approved a decree authorizing him to take the necessary measures to safeguard the Bank of Spain's gold. Initially transferred to Cartagena, the gold and silver reserves were then sent to the USSR, totaling 510 tons of precious metals worth $518 million at 1936 prices. This sum, unloaded in Odessa on November 2, was to pay for all the aid provided by Moscow, which had been greatly exaggerated. On September 26, a first cargo ship loaded with arms and ammunition, the Campeche, left Feodosia for Cartagena where it docked on October 4. On October 12, the cargo ship Komsomol landed 50 T-26 tanks in Cartagena. From October on, Soviet material aid to the republic was massive, so that by 20 December the republican air force had 30 Tupolev SB-2 Katiuska, 31 Polikarpov R.5 Rasante, 40 Polikarpov I-15 Chato, and 31 Polikarpov I-16 Mosca. In the last quarter of 1936, 106 T-26 tanks, 40 FAI self-propelled guns, BA-3 and BA-6 landed in Alicante and Cartagena.

Following the intervention of the USSR on the side of the republic, Italy and Germany were forced to revise their policy of aid to the nationalists, which until then had remained rather limited and cautious. In terms of international relations, the situation was rather delicate, since the three countries, like France and England, were members of the non-intervention committee. As we have already seen, the meeting between Hitler and Ciano in Berchtesgaden on October 24, 1936 led to a strengthening of the aid given by Berlin and Rome to the Nationalists. The recognition of Franco's government on November 18, at the initiative of Germany, left no doubt that Mussolini and Hitler were fully committed to the Caudillo.

On November 28, Italy signed a secret agreement with the Nationalists, of which Germany was immediately informed. Despite Hitler's reservations, Mussolini decided in the meeting of December 6 at Palazzo Venezia to send operational units to Spain. The three chiefs of staff (Gen. Pariani for the Army, Adm. Cavagnari for the Navy and Gen. Valle for the Air Force), Gen. Roatta, returned from Spain for the occasion, Ciano and Konteradmiral Canaris for Germany. This meeting took place after the failure of the second Nationalist offensive on Madrid and while the third, in progress for eight days, showed no sign of reaching a conclusion favorable to the insurgents. Roatta was aware that the Nationalist forces were not sufficient to break the Republicans. The Junta de defensa organized by General Miaja had managed to organize a solid defense of the capital, aided by the entry of the international brigades formed by the Comintern. Mussolini, irritated by Franco's conduct of operations, which he considered too timid, wanted to accelerate the pace in order to conclude the war as quickly as possible.

▲ General José Miaja, in charge of the defense of Madrid. (Photo credits: Archivos Estatales)

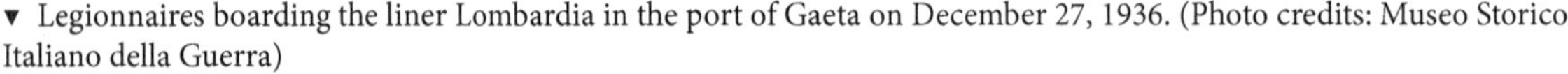

▲ Preliminary training of volunteers in Cava dei Tirreni between 7 and 27 December 1936. (Photo credit: Archivio Storico Provinciale di Bolzano)

▼ Legionnaires boarding the liner Lombardia in the port of Gaeta on December 27, 1936. (Photo credits: Museo Storico Italiano della Guerra)

▲ Legionnaires of the 3rd cp. of the 535 bis btg. Tempesta of the Div. Dio lo vuole on the tugboat that takes them aboard the Lombardia in the port of Gaeta on December 27, 1936. (Photo credit: Museo Storico Italiano della Guerra)

▼ View of Cadiz from the stern of the Lombardia on January 1, 1937. (Photo credits: Museo Storico Italiano della Guerra)

Consequently, the minutes of the meeting of December 6 specified the measures to be taken to reinforce Italy's aid to the Nationalists: first, to combat maritime traffic to Republican ports by naval and air means, and second, to reinforce air support to ground troops. While these two points were unanimously agreed upon between Rome and Berlin, the question of land units was more delicate. While Rome wanted to send two divisions, one Italian and one German, this proposal found little support in Berlin, except from Göring. Germany was primarily concerned with the economic benefits of war and did not want to damage the rearmament effort it had undertaken by diverting too much materiel to the Iberian Peninsula. However, Mussolini decided to go it alone on the issue of sending an expeditionary force. The Italian general staff wanted to give up sending reinforcements in fits and starts and demanded a massive intervention in order to influence the conduct of operations. Although there were still many differences of opinion at the end of the December 6 meeting, it clarified the division of tasks between the German and Italian air forces. The former was to concentrate on bombing, while the latter was to ensure air superiority and operations on the Balearic Islands.

On December 7, Mussolini appointed Roatta to command all Italian land and air forces in Spain, except for the Balearic Islands. It should be noted that in all matters relating to the intervention in Spain, Pietro Badoglio, chief of the General Staff, continued to be kept out of all decisions and was informed only of the minimum necessary. On the same day, Roatta informed the Chief of Staff of the MMIS, Col. Emilio Faldella, of Rome's willingness to send officers, NCOs and enlisted men to Spain to train and supervise mixed Italian-Spanish units. Since the amount of work required to train these units for Operation WHO was well beyond the capabilities of a ministerial cabinet, the

▲ Road in Cádiz leading to the Cuartel d'Infanteria, used on January 2, 1937 by Legionnaires landing from the Lombardy. (Photo credits: Museo Storico Italiano della Guerra)

SMRE was charged with organizing transportation, gathering supplies, managing payrolls, drafting administrative regulations, dealing with the issue of communications with the families of the dead and wounded, and censorship. On December 9, Faldella presented Franco with the Italian proposal for the formation of the mixed units. Although he was not very enthusiastic, Franco could not refuse, since the lower-level mixed units had performed very well in the November operations around Madrid.

Initially, Franco simply asked Italy to send company and platoon commanders so that the higher-level units would be commanded by Spaniards. But on 15 December, Italy obtained that the brigade commanders and some regimental and battalion commanders be transalpine. On December 10, while negotiations were underway, Mussolini ordered the head of the "S" section of the Ministry of Foreign Affairs, Ambassador Pietromarchi, to send 3,000 volunteers to the Iberian peninsula as soon as possible. It was Faldella's job to break the news to Franco, who did not hide his displeasure at not being involved in the decision, but nevertheless accepted the offer and decided to distribute these volunteers among the banderas of the Tercio Extranjero and the Spanish infantry regiments. Franco could not afford to refuse Mussolini's help: he knew that he urgently needed men for the offensive on Madrid. But at the same time, he did not want to give the impression that he was at the beck and call of Germany and Italy. On December 25, the formations of the Phalange and the requetès were placed under the orders of the military commands, which imposed on them the same discipline and rules in force in the regular units of the Nationalist Army. On December 12, upon his return from Italy, Roatta spoke with Franco. Together they decided to form two mixed Italian-Spanish brigades. As for the 3,000 volunteers wanted by Mussolini, they would be placed in

▲ Crowd greeting Legionnaires on the Cadiz-Seville-Huelva route on January 5, 1937. (Photo credits: Museo Storico Italiano della Guerra)

autonomous companies of the Tercio. For each of the two mixed brigades, Italy had to provide 130 officers, 150 non-commissioned officers and 1,600 soldiers, most of whom were specialized. On December 18, the first 3,446 CCN volunteers embarked on the liner Lombardia in the port of Gaeta. The volunteers' motivations were ideological, as nationalists were seen, through propaganda, as a bulwark against communism and anarchism, but also for financial gain, a taste for adventure and, for officers, for promotion. On January 14, 1937, Hermann Göring arrived in Rome to discuss ways to help Franco. During the meeting at Palazzo Venezia with Mussolini, Ciano, Pariani, Cavagnari and Valle, both sides reaffirmed their willingness to support the nationalists, while limiting their contribution so as not to lead to a European conflict. Göring assured them that Germany would provide more equipment and specialized personnel, but not combat troops. Mussolini was torn between his desire to see German troops support the Nationalists and his fear of the Reich's growing influence in the Mediterranean. In the end, it was the second sentiment that prevailed, and the Duce did not insist on sending troops to Göring. The two men decided to inform Franco of the decisions made during this meeting, including an inventory of the troops and equipment that would be sent shortly. If the flow of reinforcements sent from Italy remained rather low until November 1936, things accelerated beginning in mid-December.

Between December 18, 1936 and February 18, 1937, 48,823 volunteers arrived in Spain, 29,006 of them from the MVSN and 19,817 from the Army. The sending of such a large number of men in the space of two months was motivated by the ongoing discussions within the Non-Intervention Committee on the question of foreign volunteers.

FORMATION OF THE FIRST ITALIAN GROUND UNITS

On December 27, 1936, Roatta asked Franco for permission to form exclusively Italian battalions (banderas). Although the Caudillo was against the use of foreign units in order not to claim Republican propaganda, he was forced to accept, given the imperative need of the Nationalist Army to form reserves. With the establishment of the Italian units, Mussolini put himself in a position to have more influence on the decisions of the Nationalist command. The 49,000 men, all volunteers, sent to Spain between December 1936 and February 1937 made it possible to form five brigades, the infantry division Volontari del Littorio and various minor units. The soldiers were accompanied by a large amount of equipment, especially since the beasts of burden had been replaced by vehicles. For their transportation, the Regia Marina chartered eight liners already used for the invasion of Ethiopia (Calabria, Liguria, Lombardy, Sannio, Sardinia, Sicily, Tiber and Tuscany), three cargo ships (Antonietta, Ernani and Lodoletta), the hospital ship Helouan and 31 cargo ships already chartered by the Ferrovie dello Stato and used to transport coal from Northern Europe. The first group of volunteers was assembled in the CC.NN. special battalion group in the vicinity of Naples on 7 December 1936 for a brief period of preliminary training. The first group of 3,446 men embarked at Gaeta was drawn from this group and immediately replaced. Arriving at Cadiz on 22 December, these first volunteers formed the I brg. volunteers commanded by Gen. Rossi. The second group of 3,508 men, transported from Lombardy and landed in Cadiz on January 1, 1937, participated in the creation of the II brg. volunteers under the command of Gen. Coppi and the III brigade volunteers of Gen. Nuvolini. Once the training activity was over, and after renewing the personnel several times due to departures, the CC.NN. special battalions was disbanded on February 5, 1937.

▲ Ground personnel and Fiat CR.32 at Torrijos airport in 1936. (Photo credits: Bolesani family)

▼ CR.32 formation from La Cucaracha in the Madrid sector in November 1936. (Photo credits: Dequal family)

THE RISE OF THE AIR FORCE

As seen above, the first action of Soviet planes in Spain was carried out on October 28, 1936 by four Tupolev SB-2 bombers of Grupo No. 12, which attacked the airfield of Tablada. These modern planes had a higher top speed than the Fiat CR.32s, which had to implement a new interception technique. The next day, three CR.32s attacked three SB-2s in a dive near Valdemoro. Nationalist pilot Salas claimed to have shot down a bomber, which seemed to be confirmed by observers on the ground. On November 2, a raid by 10 SB-2s on Talavera damaged 6 CR.32s, and Maj. Fagnani decided to redeploy 14 CR.32s to Torrijos the next day. Also on November 2, s.Lt. Mantelli and m.llo Sozzi shot down an SB-2 of the 2nd escuadrilla SB based in San Clemente in the Murcia area. This was the first confirmed Italian victory against this type of aircraft, achieved thanks to the 5000 m altitude from which the Fiats attacked their target located 2000 m below.

On November 3, the Aniene arrived in Seville after moving up the Guadalquivir to unload 21 CR.32s and 4 Ro.37s. The new fighters formed the 3rd escuadrilla de caza under the command of Capt. Mosca. Formed in Tablada, the squadron reached Torrijos on November 9, joining the 18 CR.32 then operating at this airport. The 2 squadrons that joined allowed the constitution of a fighter group formed on November 11 and commanded by Maj. Tarcisio Fagnani. The 1st escuadrilla of Capt. Dequal remained based in Seville-Tablada with 11 operational CR.32.

On November 4, the CR.32 of Cpl. Dequal and Sgt. Magistrini were on patrol over the airfield at Getafe, near Madrid, to cover Nationalist troops. Pursuing two SB-2s, the Fiat arrived at Cuatro Vientos airfield just as a squadron of Polikarpov I-15s was returning from a parade over Madrid. The Italians managed to break free, but as they passed over the Nationalist lines, Dequal noticed a lone Ro.37 bis fighting with seven Polikarpov I-15s commanded by Kapitan Pavel Richagov. The intervention of the Fiat biplanes saved the Ro.37 bis, but the two fighters were shot down. Dequal jumped with his parachute into the Republican lines and managed to return to the territory under Nationalist control. Magistrini, on the other hand, was killed in the first battle between Italian airmen and Soviet I-15 biplanes.

▲ Col. Bonomi's S.81 damaged by the SB-2 attack on the Talavera de la Reina airfield on November 25, 1936. (Photo credit: Museo Caproni)

▲ Tupolev SB-2 damaged at the Nationalist airfield of Logroño-Agoncillo in 1936. (Photo credit: Fernando Pina Rubio collection on AviationCorner.net)

▼ Launch of a Republican Polikarpov I-15 using a Ford V8 equipped with a compressor. (Photo credit: Patrick Laureau Collection)

▲ Ro.37 bis of the National Air Force. (Photo credits: Anderle family)

▼ Bombing near the Toledo bridge, Madrid, November 1936. The truck on the right is a ZiS-5.

On November 5, 9 CR.32 commanded by Corporal Carlo Albero Maccagno on an escort mission for 3 Ro.37 bis were attacked by 15 I-15 near Leganés. Maccagno was shot down but managed to parachute over Madrid. He was wounded in the leg and had to be amputated. On the opposite side, two I-15s did not return to their base: that of Lieutenant Mitrofanov, the first Soviet pilot to be killed in Spain, and a second plane destroyed while attempting a crash landing on the paseo de la Castellana.

On November 10, a new adversary appeared in the skies over Madrid: the Polikarpov I-16 monoplane fighter. The CR.32 faced it for the first time on November 15: 15 transalpine biplanes faced 4 I-16s and shot down Vladimir N. Vzorov's plane. Despite its greater speed, the Polikarpov monoplane lacked the maneuverability of the CR.32, whose pilots engaged in circle combat. However, the arrival of the I-15 and I-16 in Spanish skies marked the end of the CR.32's technological superiority.

On November 19 a massive raid took place against the university sector of Madrid, with 4 S.81, 18 Ju 52 and 12 Ro.37 escorted by 16 CR.32 and 9 He 51. The Nationalist formation was attacked by I-15 and I-16 that claimed to have destroyed 3 Ju 52 and 3 fighters. In reality, only one Ju 52 was shot down. The Nationalists claimed 7 victories, while Republican losses were one I-16 and one I-15 shot down, both attributed to Italian fighters. Air battles over Madrid were daily, and claims by both sides were almost always exaggerated.

On November 25, the Talavera camp was attacked by Republican artillery in the morning and by 6 SB-2s in the afternoon, which seriously damaged the S.81 at Col. Bonomi and 2 Ro.37s. As a consequence, 6 Ro.37 were redeployed to Caceres. The construction of a new airfield was also undertaken at Velada, 15 km west of Talavera. As Madrid's anti-aircraft defense became more powerful, Ju 52 and S.81 attacks were increasingly carried out at night.

▲ Italian airmen enjoy a lunch on Dec. 25, 1936 in Tablada. (Photo credits: Dequal family)

▲ Polikarpov I-15 Chato of the Republican Air Force.

▼ Maj. Prospero Nuvoli in the center and Cpl. Dequal on the right at Tablada in December 1936. (Photo credit: Dequal family)

On December 2, the new airfield at Velada was targeted by a raid of 18 R-5 Polikarpovs that damaged 3 S.81s. The 2 CR.32 of the surveillance patrol, including that of s.Lt. Cenni, managed to take off and shot down 3 of the attackers. On December 4, 2 R-5s returning from an attack on the Navalmoral airfield were shot down over Torrijos by CR.32s, one of which was piloted by Sergeant Baschirotto.

On December 5, Escuadrillas 2a and 3a were transferred to Barcience, only a few kilometers east of Torrijos but with a better runway. On December 5 and 6, CR.32s escorted Ro.37s operating in the Casa de Campo sector. On this occasion, 2 I-16s and an I-15 were shot down while Sgt. Ferrari's CR.32 was hit and forced to make a crash landing.

On December 20, a fight between Fiat CR.32s and Polikarpov I-15s resulted in the loss of three of the latter. The next day, Col. Bonomi returned to Italy and was replaced by Col. Vicenzo Velardo as head of the Italian air force in Spain. On 28 December 1936, the Aviación del Tercio ceased to exist and was replaced by the Aviazione Legionaria.

▲ Italian and Spanish ground crew posing in front of a CR.32. (Photo credits: Comelli family)
▼ Polikarpov I-16, nicknamed "Fly" by the Republicans and "Rat" by the Nationalists.

NAVAL INTERVENTION

From the beginning, the Italian navy played a decisive role in the Spanish conflict. Starting on September 30, a mission to escort Italian transatlantic ships in transit through Gibraltar was established, which justified the deployment of units of the Regia Marina in Tangier. The first sorties were carried out by the light cruiser Bande Nere and by the destroyers Pancaldo and Da Recco, which were respectively replaced by Pigafetta and Da Mosto on October 4. The day before, the Bande Nere had been replaced by the Da Barbiano, which carried a unit of the San Marco btg. that was to remain in Tangier for more than a year.

In addition to the ships assigned to protect traffic in the Strait of Gibraltar, Italy sent ships to the main ports in Republican hands to protect its citizens and diplomatic missions. The cruisers Di Giussano and Pola were sent to Barcelona, the latter arriving on September 5 and departing on September 11 for Palma de Mallorca, where it remained until October 3. The Di Giussano was replaced by the Colleoni, which docked in Barcelona on the morning of September 6. On September 11 it was joined by the Usodimare to replace the Pessagno. The Usodimare left the Catalan capital on September 29, while the Di Giussano returned to La Spezia on October 4. She was replaced by the Eugenio di Savoia, which had arrived two days earlier. In Alicante, the Regia Marina employed the old light cruiser Quarto from September 9. Following threats to the Italian consulate in Almeria, the destroyer Da Verazzano, which had arrived in Alicante on October 16, was sent there between October 23 and 25. During these two days, the commander, C.F. Gaetano Catalano Gonzaga, obtained assurances that the consulate would not be occupied. After taking aboard 14 Italians, a German and a Spanish political prisoner, the ship made a brief stop in the port of Cartagena to inform Adm. Div. Vittorio Tur, commander of the Italian naval units in Spain, of the state of the Republican fleet.

▲ International squadron anchored in Tangier in mid-September 1936.

▲ The destroyers Antonio Pigafetta (in the foreground) and Alvise da Mosto in front of Tangier in October 1936.

▼ The light cruiser Alberico da Barbiano at anchor in Tangier on October 10, 1936. (Photo credit: Franco Bargoni collection)

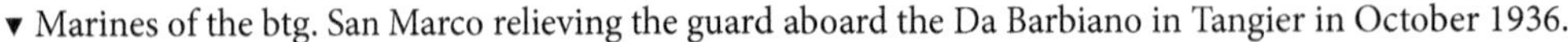

▲ The Da Barbiano escorting the liner Conte Biancamano through the Strait of Gibraltar on October 13, 1936.

▼ Marines of the btg. San Marco relieving the guard aboard the Da Barbiano in Tangier in October 1936.

Even though the protection and, if necessary, the evacuation of citizens were good pretexts for sending military ships to Spain, the presence of the Regia Marina ships made it possible to gather information on merchant ships leaving or bound for Republican ports and their cargoes. However, towards the middle of October, the presence of Italian units in the republican ports became more and more delicate due to the hostility shown by a part of the population. The Italian command even feared an attack by uncontrolled Republican ships or submarines. It therefore decided to replace the most modern ships with older or secondary units. On October 20, the San Giorgio arrived in Barcelona to replace the Eugenio di Savoia as the flagship. Adm. Div. Vittorio Tur was replaced by Contramm. Angelo Iachino as commander of the Italian naval forces in Spain. With Italy's recognition of the Nationalist government on 18 November, ships of the Regia Marina left Republican ports. The San Giorgio left Barcelona the following day, calling at Palma de Mallorca from 20 to 23

▲ Adm.Div. Vittorio Tur, accompanied by Consul Bossi (left), visiting Vice President Cassol at the Generalidad de Barcelona on October 2, 1936. (Photo credits: Franco Bargoni collection)

before reaching La Maddelana on 25. In Tangier, the Da Barbiano was replaced by the Quarto on 18 November, which became the flagship of the Italian Naval Group in the ports near the Straits commanded by Contramm. Alberto Marenco di Moriondo.

At the end of October 1936, as Soviet naval traffic in the Mediterranean increased, surveillance of the Strait of Sicily and the Strait of Messina was intensified. Between 28 October and 2 November, the destroyers Borea and Nembo carried out two surveillance missions each, with the aim of signaling the passage of Russian or Republican ships to Nationalist auxiliary cruisers. They were joined at the beginning of November by the destroyers Strale, Dardo and Freccia. During the sortie between 3 and 4 November, the Strale identified and followed the Russian freighter Komsomol, which was sunk on 14 December by the cruiser Canarias. Between October 28 and November 6, Italian ships identified 51 merchant vessels. However, the surveillance missions in the Sicilian Channel were interrupted because the reports were not followed up, as the nationalist ships were too few to intervene in time.

To advise the Nationalist Navy, which lacked officers and had only elementary organization, Rome sent C.V. Giovanni Ferretti (aka Dr. Rossi) as a liaison officer with naval force commander Francisco Moreno. He arrived in Cadiz via Tangier, Tetouan and Seville on October 3. His first task was to create a trilingual cipher code to allow collaboration between the Nationalist, German and Italian navies. He was then involved in negotiations between the Nationalist Navy and Rome to provide two submarines to fight more effectively against the merchant ships supplying the Republican ports. At the beginning of November, confident of a positive response from Rome, Ferretti prepared to the last detail the arrival of the submarines in the arsenal of Carraca, in the province of Cadiz. But his efforts were in vain, since in mid-November the Regia Marina decided to operate its submarines from bases on the mainland, refusing for the moment any transfer.

▲ Adm.Div. Vittorio Tur greets Admiral Rolf Carls upon his arrival aboard the Graf Spee in Barcelona in October 1936.

▲ The Bartolomeo Colleoni, bearing the mark of Admiral Goiran, at anchor off Barcelona in the second half of September 1936. (Photo credit: A. de Toro collection)

▼ View of the port of Tangier at the end of 1936. In the foreground the Quarto and, behind it, a French destroyer of the Vauquelin class (Photo credits: Franco Bargoni collection)

The first clandestine submarine campaign of the Civil War, which ended on December 4, 1936, involved the submarines Naiade, Topazio, Sciesa and Torricelli based at La Maddalena. Each unit embarked a Nationalist liaison officer to identify targets. On November 22, 1936, the Torricelli torpedoed the Republican light cruiser Miguel de Cervantes off Cartagena, seriously damaging its stern. Towed back to port, the ship remained unavailable for repairs until 11 April 1938. The republican commission of inquiry blamed a German submarine, while the British Admiralty attributed the torpedoing to a Spanish submarine belonging to the Nationalists. The torpedoing of the Cervantes had an enormous impact that went far beyond the material damage caused to the ship. The effect on the morale of the Republican crews, who had previously thought that the enemy had no submarines, was disastrous. On the Italian side, however, there was fear of the potential consequences if the truth came to light, and further restrictions were placed on submarine commanders to fire torpedoes only in cases of extreme necessity. Frustration became the norm among the crews, who became accustomed to abortive attack maneuvers.

Despite the operational limits imposed, the increase in naval intervention was ratified at the meeting of December 6. During this month, 11 submarines were sent on missions, to no avail, most of the attacks were not completed. However, the threat of a submarine attack and the action of the few Republican surface units forced the Republican fleet to remain in their bases and the Soviet ships to abandon the Mediterranean routes.

▲ The Eugene of Savoy in front of Barcelona in early October 1936. (Photo credits: Franco Bargoni collection)

The Russian freighter Komsomol en route to Barcelona photographed by the Strale off Cape Bon on November 4, 1936. (Photo credit: Franco Bargoni collection)

The nationalist cruiser Canarias that sank the Komsomol on December 14, 1936.

ITALIANS ON THE REPUBLICAN FRONT

Antifascist Italians who had taken refuge in France and Switzerland were among the first foreign volunteers to come to Spain to support the republic. The first mention of a formation of Italian volunteers dates back to August 3, 1936 and refers to an Italian group incorporated into the Columna 19 de Julio of the PSUC militia. These were probably volunteers from the Italian community living in Barcelona. Carlo Rosselli, one of the founders of the antifascist movement Giustizia e Libertà, created the Colonna Italiana Rosselli (or batallón Giacomo Matteoti) on August 17, 1936, which numbered between 130 and 150 men. Attached to the Columna Ascaso, an anarchist formation commanded by Domingo Ascaso and Gregorio Jover, the Colonna Italiana Rosselli fought from August 28 on the Aragon front, repelling a Nationalist attack on Mount Pelato, between the towns of Huesca and Almudévar.

Some of the Italian exiles in France decided to form a battalion with the name Garibaldi on October 26, 1936, commanded by Republican Randolfo Pacciardi, assisted by political commissar Antonio Roasio of the PCI. With about 800 men and aggregated to the XII brigada internacional, the battalion received its baptism of fire on November 12, 1936 during the fighting at Cerro de Los Angeles.

The leader of the PCI in exile, Palmiro Togliatti, an influential member of the Comintern, also went to Spain where he became one of the main advisors to the PCE.

▲ The Republican cruiser Miguel de Cervantes, torpedoed on November 22, 1936 by the submarine Torricelli. (Photo credits: Franco Bargoni collection)

III: THE CONQUEST OF MALAGA

In early 1937, the capture of the Malaga crossing, the first operation of the Civil War conducted primarily by Italian legionnaires, was the only major victory for the Nationalist camp.

OBJECTIVE: MALAGA

By the end of 1936, the Nationalists controlled 60% of mainland Spain, Spanish Morocco, the Canary Islands and the Balearic Islands, with the exception of Menorca. However, the entire Mediterranean coast remained in Republican territory and was the main gateway for Soviet military aid. In order to have a port on the Mediterranean coast, Franco implemented the capture of Malaga, in Andalusia, his first objective after the capture of Madrid.

The initiative to carry out the conquest of Malaga as an action independent of that of Madrid was taken by Gen. Mario Roatta, who informed Franco on December 17, 1936. As seen above, the Caudillo was not enthusiastic about the idea of Italian-led units fighting on Spanish soil, but the failure of his third offensive on the Madrid front and the lack of nationalist troops led him to accept the Italian offensive on Malaga. He also hoped that the attack on Malaga would force the Republicans to send reinforcements from Madrid. The halting of the fourth offensive on the capital in mid-January 1937 due to particularly unfavorable weather conditions prompted Franco, who until then had

▲ Entry of Franco's troops into Malaga on February 8, 1937.

▲ Gen. Vincenzo Velardo, first commander of the Legionary Aviation.

▼ S.81 of the XXIV Gr. in flight over Andalusia in February 1937. (Photo credit: Museo Caproni Taliedo)

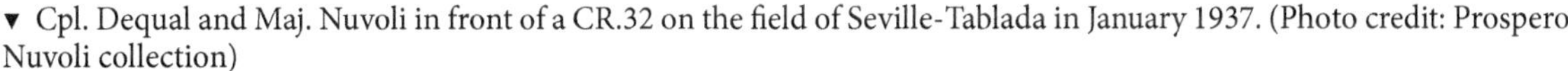

▲ The Aniene en route to Seville, escorted by the destroyer Aquila, late December 1936. (Photo credits: Bernardo Monti collection)

▼ Cpl. Dequal and Maj. Nuvoli in front of a CR.32 on the field of Seville-Tablada in January 1937. (Photo credit: Prospero Nuvoli collection)

been less than enthusiastic, to revise his position on the action against Malaga. He understood the diversionary effect it could have on the Republicans and decided to prepare it together with the fifth offensive against Madrid. But the offensive on Malaga did not have the hoped-for effect on Madrid's defenses, and the February 1937 offensive in the Jarama Valley was another failure for Franco.

For Roatta, the capture of Malaga was of fundamental importance in reducing the route of supplies from Italy, which until then had to cross the Strait of Gibraltar and land at Cadiz. In addition, he wanted to demonstrate to Franco the operational capabilities of the Italian expeditionary corps. On December 22, 1936, Roatta presented his project to Queipo de Llano, in charge of the southern front. Having obtained his approval, he went on a reconnaissance mission to the Malaga sector on December 23 and 24 with Col. Emilio Faldella, chief of staff of the MMIS, to study offensive planning. Three routes were considered for the attack: Granada-Motril, Loja-Malaga and Antequera-Malaga. The first route was the most profitable, since it would isolate the entire Republican salient of Malaga, between Órgiva and Estepona, attacking from the east, but would require mountain warfare in the Sierra Nevada to secure the sides of the road. The other two routes offered the opportunity for convergent action on Malaga, but allowed only the occupation of half the Republican salient, which nevertheless concentrated 4/5 of the forces deployed there. On the recommendation of Faldella, who knew well the topographical difficulties of the first route, Roatta excluded an offensive on Motril. The other attack routes were not without natural obstacles, Malaga being surrounded by a mountainous cirque that facilitated its defense, and the access routes crossing steep valleys.

On December 25, Roatta gathered at the Madrid Hotel in Seville the officers of the MMIS and the officers supervising the first contingent of 3446 CC.NN. that had landed in Cadiz on December 22. He appointed Col. Mario Guassardo as commander of the 1st mixed brg. and assured the cadre officers that their men would fight in all-Italian units.

On December 26, Roatta went to Salamanca accompanied by Faldella to meet Franco. The latter accepted the constitution of Italian units and gave his final agreement for the operation against

▲ The Sanctuary of the Virgen de la Cabeza besieged by the Republicans between September 14, 1936 and May 1, 1937.

Malaga. On December 28, Roatta went to Rome to inform Franco of his decision and to ask for the necessary reinforcements. The next day, Ciano telegraphed a note to the MMIS authorizing the operation against Malaga and announcing the arrival of new battalions.

On December 31, Faldella circulated three documents to the MMIS regarding the plan of action on Malaga, reflecting the blitzkrieg doctrine then in effect in the Italian army. The offensive was to be based on mass actions in rapid succession against decisive objectives located deep within the enemy position. The selected starting bases were concentrated in the Antequera-Archidona-Loja sector, as close as possible to the objectives. In order to achieve the surprise effect, reconnaissance activities were to be reduced to the bare minimum, no artillery preparation would be made and diversionary action would be conducted on D-2. Speed of maneuver would be assured by the availability of reserve transport vehicles. Upon his return from Rome on 10 January 1937, Roatta accepted Faldella's directives.

CREATION AND STRENGTHENING OF THE LEGIONARY AIR FORCE

Before examining the course of the operation against Malaga, it is worth returning to the creation of the Legionary Air Force, which was to intervene in the fighting. As we have already seen, the Legionary Air Force was officially created on December 28, 1936 under the command of Vincenzo Velardo, who had arrived from Italy with the rank of colonel and was promoted to general in order to reinforce his prestige with the Spanish generals.

The reinforcement of the Italian air force in Spain continued with the arrival of 9 Savoia S.81 of the 13th Sq. of the XXVI Gr. on December 29. On January 1, 1937, the commercial ship Aniene docked in Seville with 20 Fiat CR.32 bis, 3 Romeo Ro.41 and the personnel of 2 fighter squadrons. On 15 January, 9 more S.81 of the 11th Sq. landed in Seville. Redistributed to Soria with the 9 three-engine aircraft arrived on December 29, they formed the XXIV Gr. Marelli heavy bombardment commanded by Col. Ferdinando Raffaelli.

▲ Franco's soldiers on the coastal road to Estepona on January 12, 1937.

▲ José Villalba Rubio in 1924, then commander of the 3rd bandera de la Legión.

In mid-January 1937 the Legionary Aviation deployed 16 S.81 of the XXIV Marelli Group, 21 Ro.37bis of the 1st and 2nd squares, 69 Fiat CR.32 and 3 Ro.41 of the I Cucaracha Group (1st, 2nd and 3rd squares) and of the II Cucaracha Group (4th, 5th and 6th squares).

On January 22, the port of Cadiz, where Italian troops were landing, was attacked by 3 Tupolev SB-2. The intervention of 2 CR.32s on patrol over the city forced the Soviet bombers to get rid of their bombs before reaching their target and to return as soon as possible to their lines, pursued unsuccessfully by the CR.32s for more than 100 km. On January 28, the hurricane that hit Seville damaged 4 S.81s on the makeshift airfield of La Cascajera, used for fear of SB-2 raids on Tablada.

On January 29, 9 CR.32s of the 5th Squadron escorted 3 S.81s and 3 Ro.37 bis entrusted by the Nationalists to supply the shrine of the Virgen de la Cabeza in the Sierra de Andújar, which was under siege by the Republicans. Weather conditions quickly deteriorated and soon the pilots lost visual contact with the other aircraft in their formation due to the appearance of thick fog. Six CR.32s crashed, two pilots were killed and four others were taken prisoner.

On February 4, the Aniene landed in Seville with 12 Fiat CR.32s and 11 pilots under the command of Cpl. Mario Viola.

NATIONALIST OFFENSIVE AND ITALIAN PREPARATIONS

While the Italian offensive was still being prepared, Queipo de Llano ordered Colonel Francisco Borbón y de la Torre, Duke of Seville, to launch a local attack in the western sector of the Malaga salient, along the coastal road. On January 14, the Nationalist forces captured Estepona, and then

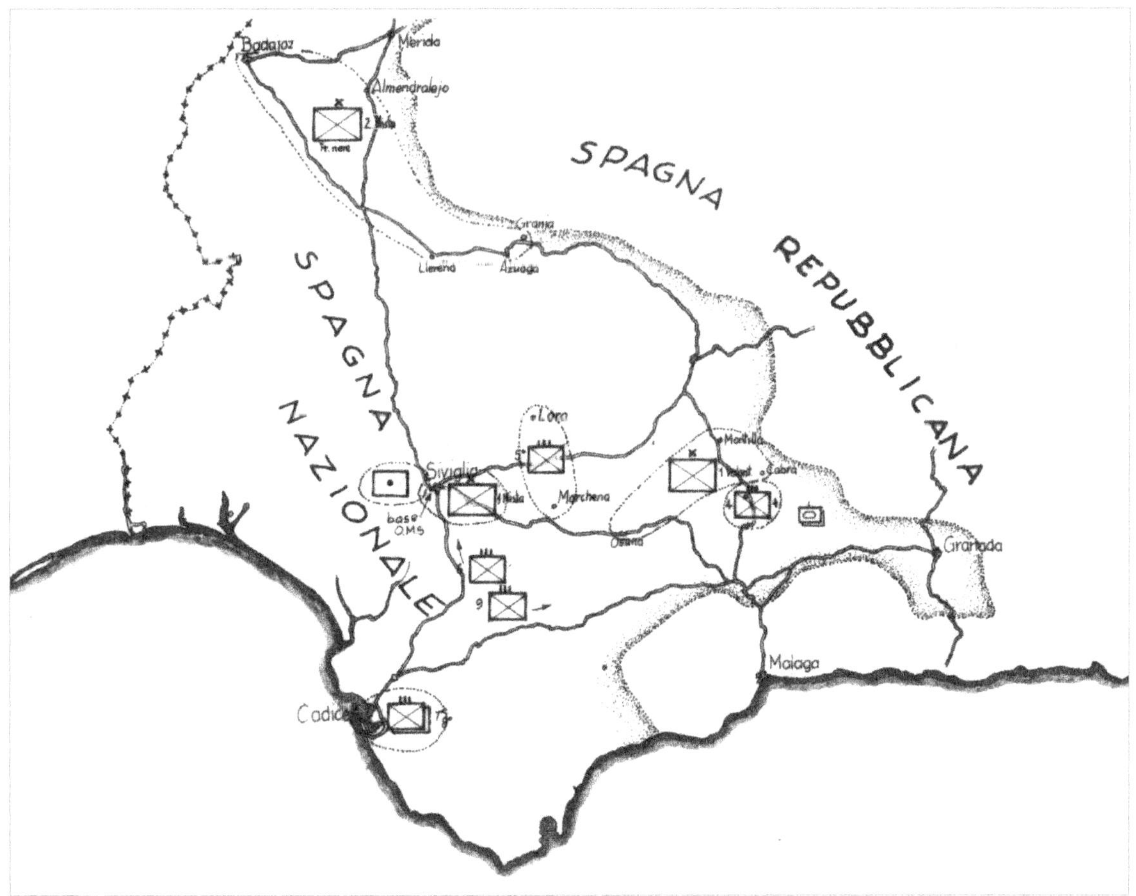

▲ Position of the Italian units on January 31, 1937.

continued their advance on San Pedro de Alcàntara, which they took on the 15th, and on Marbella, which they reached on January 17 without encountering any resistance. At the same time, at the other end of the Malaga salient, a Nationalist column from Granada commanded by Colonel Antonio Muñoz Jiménez occupied Alhama on January 22. This advance offered a new route for the attack on Malaga, via Vélez-Malaga. Roatta decided to take advantage of this opportunity and divided his forces into 3 columns to invest a front of more than 130 km.

On January 24, Roatta sent a telegram to Ciano to update him on the latest developments and the difficulties encountered in the preparations. Because of the Nationalist offensives on the flanks of the Malaga salient, Roatta feared that the surprise effect of the Italian attack would be compromised. The offensive against Malaga was in fact no longer an open secret, widely reported in the Anglo-Saxon press. But the republican command could not count on any help from the Valencian government, since the coastal road was interrupted at Motril due to a flood. Roatta also had to deal with the almost total lack of training of the first troops to arrive in Spain, due to the urgency with which they were assembled and sent to the theater of operations. In addition, the units lacked cohesion or esprit de corps, being composed of elements from different corps and units of the militia or army. Despite this, Roatta believed he could launch his offensive on February 1, the anniversary of the founding of the MVSN, but he did not rule out a delay of a few days. This last point displeased Ciano, who informed Faldella, who was in Rome at the time, asking for new reinforcements. Franco was also eager to see the Italian units in action, hoping for a victory that would restore the morale of the Nationalist troops stranded in front of Madrid.

On January 26, Roatta gave the order to deploy the units in their assembly areas, namely the Osuna-Aguadulce sectors for the right column commanded by Col. Carlo Rivolta, Aguilar de la Frontera-Montilla for the central column of Gen. Edmondo Rossi and Lucena-Cabra for the left column of Col. Mario Guassardo. Located on average 60 km from the Malaga salient, these assembly areas were chosen to leave the area of the offensive in doubt.

For his attack, code-named Lightning, Roatta had about 10,000 men distributed among the following units:

- I gr. banderas composed of the banderas Aquila, Carroccio and Leone (1 bandera is equivalent to 1 battalion and a banderas group to 1 regiment);
- II gr. banderas composed of the banderas Folgore, Indomito and Falco;
- III gr. banderas composed of the banderas Hurricane, Arrow, Storm and Wolves;
- IV gr. banderas composed of the banderas Buffalo, Bull and Bison;
- 1st and 2nd cp. assault tanks out of 13 L 3 each;
- 1 platoon of the 3rd assault tank cp;
- 1 armored car company on 8 Lancia 1ZM ;
- 1st cp. m.m. ;
- I and II gr. 105/28 guns on 2 batteries of 3 pieces each;
- II gr. 149/12 howitzers on 2 batteries ;
- 1st btr. 75/27 CK guns ;
- 1st and 2nd btr. 20/65 Breda guns ;
- 1 section of 2 guns of 47/32 ;
- 3 engineer platoons;
- 2 platoons of telephone liaison engineers;
- 1 section of radiotelegraph engineers;
- 1 platoon of engineers.

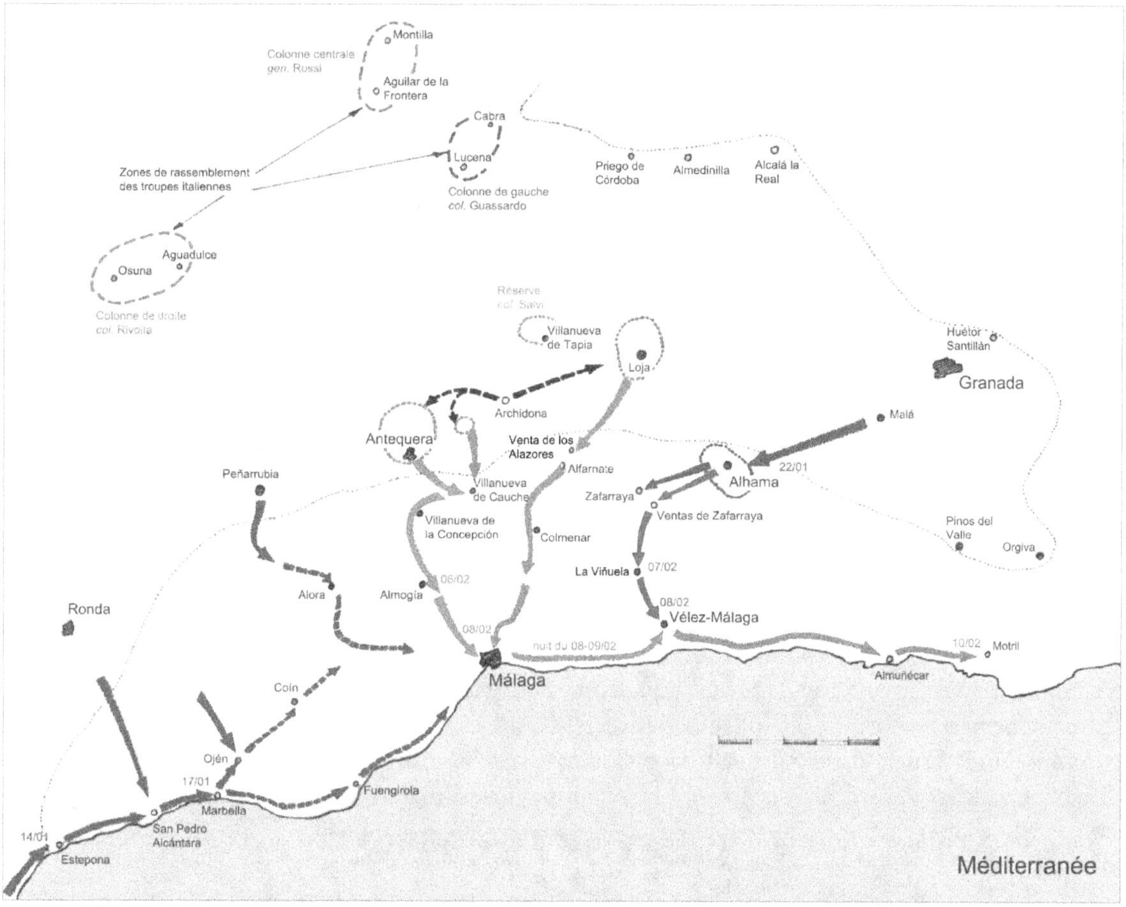

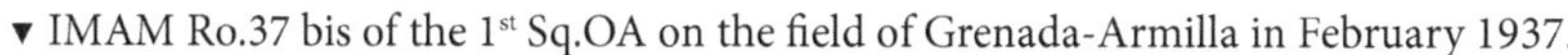

▲ Map of the operations against the Malaga salient between January 14 and February 10, 1937. (Credits: Aymeric López)

▼ IMAM Ro.37 bis of the 1st Sq.OA on the field of Grenada-Armilla in February 1937.

Transportation of the troops would be provided by 720 vehicles. On the evening of February 4, the II gr. 100/17 howitzers, formed two days earlier, arrived in Loja to join the Italian troops. To counter any attack behind his position, Roatta sent the V banderas, including the Implacable and Ardente banderas, to provide cover in the Lucena sector.

The Italian force was supplemented at both ends of the front by Nationalist forces that provided flank protection in accordance with agreements made on January 30 with Queipo de Llano. The right flank was covered by four battalions of the 2nd Division under Colonel Francisco Borbón y de la Torre from Marbella and Ronda, while the left flank was covered by an infantry battalion of the Regimiento de Infantería Cádiz n° 33 and a company of regulars deployed in Alhama under Colonel Antonio Muñoz Jiménez. Colonel Basilio León Maestre was in charge of the reserve troops. In total, the Nationalist forces numbered about 10,000 men.

From the sea, the Francoists could count on the assistance of the cruisers Canarias and Almirante Cervera. For air support, the Legionary Air Force transferred some units from the Madrid front to Andalusia. The 3rd and 4th Sq. on CR.32 and 5 Ro.37 of the 1st Sq. were reassigned to the Seville-Tablada airfield, where 13 S.81 of the XXIV Gr. were already located. A total of 36 CR.32 participated in the operation. The Nationalist Air Force intervened with the 12 Breguet XIX of the 3-G-10 and 4-G-10 squadrons, a squadron of Junkers 52 and the 3 CR.32s of Joaquín García Morato's Patrulla Azul.

Facing this force, the Republicans had 12,000 men in the front line and 8,000 in reserve, including militiamen from different factions, men from the Guardia de Asalto and soldiers from the regular army, armed with only 10,000 rifles, between 70 and 80 machine guns, about 20 mortars and 16 cannons. On February 3, 6 Soviet self-propelled cannons BA-6 and FAI were sent as reinforcements. The command of the sector was assumed by Colonel José Villalba Rubio, who had just been trans-

▲ From left to right, Sergeant Camoni, s.Lt. Mantelli, Sgt. Colauzzi, Sgt. Salvi and, first on the right, Sgt. Cappellini on the field of Granada-Armilla in February 1937.

ferred from Catalonia to replace Colonel Manuel Hernández Arteaga. Resistance positions were set up on the passes, dominating the access routes and held by numerically consistent forces, but the defense system was discontinuous and the possibilities of support between sectors weak due to the lack of transportation. For anti-aircraft defense, the Loyalists could only count on one cannon and three machine guns. The republicans' air support was limited: it consisted of 12 Polikarpov I-15, 6 Tupolev SB-2 commanded by kaptain Nikolai Ostriakov, 5 to 6 Dewoitine 371 and Nieuport Ni 52 C1 and 4 Potez 540 and 542 of the escuadrilla Malraux (the name given to the escuadrilla España from the end of November 1936 onwards) redeployed from Teruel.

The transport of the Italian troops to their assembly areas by rail was completed on January 30, one day later than planned. On January 31, Roatta summoned the staff officers, generals, and colonels involved in the offensive to Puente Genil. He gave them orders on the deployment to the bases of departure, on the progress of the attack on Malaga, on the implementation of air and naval support and on the organization and functioning of the logistic services.

ROATTA ATTACKS

The march of the Italian columns to their home bases began on the night of February 1, 1936. On February 2, a Heinkel He 70 of the Condor Legion on a photo reconnaissance mission was shot down by I-15s over Estepona. On the morning of February 3, three Nationalist battalions commanded by Colonel Francisco Borbón y de la Torre attacked the western sector of the Malaga salient from Ronda. This time they met with strong resistance. At the same time, in the sky above Loja, 6 Polikarpov I-15s engaged 3 CR.32s. Two I-15s were damaged and had to attempt a forced landing near Torremolinos, one of which was destroyed. The CR.32s of Lieutenant Larsimont and Sgt. Frattini also had to make an emergency landing and then be repaired. On the same day, Franco went

▲ Legionnaire of the right column attacking the Torcal Pass, between Antequera and Villanueva de la Concepciòn, February 5, 1937. (Photo credit: Italian Historical Museum of War)

to the headquarters established by Roatta in Iznajar. On February 4, the Caudillo visited the Italian units deployed in their bases: the column of Colonel Rivolta in Antequera, that of Gen. Rossi in Loja with a detachment in Antequera, and that of Col. Guassardo in Alhama. The reserve commanded by Col. Constantino Salvi was in the Villanueva de Tapia sector. In order to confuse the enemy and keep the area of attack uncertain, the Legionary Air Force in charge of the air support of the operation was transferred at the last moment to the airfield of Granada-Armilla. There were 19 CR.32 and 10 Ro.37, which were therefore 15 minutes from the front.

On Friday, February 5, at 6:30 a.m., the three columns went on the attack, without any artillery preparation. The reserves were transferred to Loja at the same time. The right column was the first to make contact with the Republicans. During the day, the tanks of the 2nd Cp. reached Villanueva de la Concepciòn, while the infantry was blocked by Republican resistance on the road to the Torcal pass, on Hill 860. The central column, led by the 1st Cp.m.m. and the 1st Cp. assault wagons, entered the basin of Venta de los Alazores where the soldiers, until then transported in trucks, dismounted. After deploying the artillery, the soldiers attacked the Republican positions that dominated the basin, held by 2,000 militiamen, without managing to dislodge them before nightfall. Five Ro.37 bis attacked the Republican reinforcements on the road leading from Malaga to Venta de los Alazores. The detachment of the central column from Antequera was stopped at the entrance to Villanueva de Cauche. From Alhama, the left column, which attacked at about 9:30 a.m. with a first bandera, brought a second bandera at about 12 p.m. to break through the pass defenses and open the way for the third bandera, which forced the Republican defenders to retreat. Roatta, who had risen to the front line to follow the attack, was wounded in the arm, but retained command of operations. By evening, the entire column had crossed the ridge and reached the Ventas de Zafarraya sector. At the same time, the Nationalist forces of Colonel Antonio Muñoz Jiménez advanced on Zafarraya, which they reached around 14:00. The Legionary Air Force supported the advance of the troops by carry-

▲ Intervention of Ro.37 bis on the Malaga front in the first days of February 1937. (Photo credits: Nino Bortolini collection)

Two photographs with captions.

▲ Road leading to the Torcal Pass from Antequera. (Photo credits: Sebastian Aguilar collection)

▼ The basin of Venta de los Alazores and the pass that leads to Alfarnate. (Photo credits: betanya collection)

ing out reconnaissance missions and bombing Republican positions. Ten S.81 and 19 CR.32 were assigned to attack Colmenar, but the bombing was not very accurate. The S.81s were then grounded for three days due to heavy rains that made the Seville-Tablada terrain impassable for these heavy three-engine aircraft.

By the evening of February 5, only the left column had succeeded in breaking through the Republican line of resistance. The command had two alternatives: reinforce the central column, which according to the initial plan was to carry the main effort of the attack, or shift the center of gravity of its action to the left. Aware that the conquest of Malaga was more important than that of Vélez-Malaga, Roatta opted for the first solution, although he had initially thought of reinforcing the left column with two battalions. Finally, Roatta decided at 11 o'clock in the evening to assign a reserve bandera as reinforcement to the central column.

On the morning of February 6, operations did not resume until 7:30 a.m., after the fog had cleared. The right column, sensing that the Republican forces were preparing to retreat, moved its infantry forward to join the L3s of the 2nd cp. at Villanueva de la Concepción and then continued its advance toward Almogia, which was reached at dusk. The central column managed to get out of the Venta de los Alazores basin and advanced towards Colmenar, which had already been evacuated. Then it advanced towards Puerto de Léon and Costa de Viento, where it was stopped by the Republican resistance. The left column also continued to advance from Ventas de Zafarraya beyond the junction to Riogord-Colmenar. The reserve was transferred to Venta de los Alazores in order to intervene at both Colmenar and Ventas de Zafarraya. On the west coast, the Nationalist forces of the Duke of Seville advanced without meeting much resistance at Torremolinos and captured 3 self-propelled BA-6 cannons. On the evening of February 6, only the detachment of the central column remained blocked in front of Villanueva de Cauche. Facing the Italian and Nationalist advance, Colonel Villalba ordered the evacuation of Malaga by the coastal road to Almeria.

▲ Bunker overlooking the road between Venta de los Alazores and Alfarnate. (Photo credits: Salvador collection)

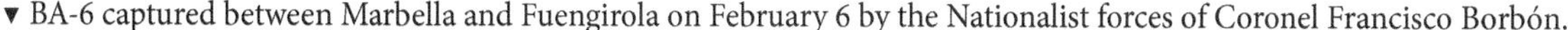

▲ L3 column advancing towards Malaga.

▼ BA-6 captured between Marbella and Fuengirola on February 6 by the Nationalist forces of Coronel Francisco Borbón.

On February 7, the right column resumed its advance at 8 a.m. and took up position on the heights overlooking Malaga that same evening, just 2.5 km from the city center. The central column, with 6 banderas, attacked the positions of Costa de Viento at 7:30 a.m., combining a frontal attack with overtaking maneuvers on the flanks. The position fell toward 12 o'clock and the central column then made contact with the right column, whose command passed into the hands of Gen. Rossi. The detachment of the central column managed to enter Villanueva de Cauche while the Nationalist forces of the Duke of Seville reached the mouth of the Guadalhorce, supported by the fire of the cruisers Canarias and Almirante Cervera and the gunboats Canalejas and Canovas del Castillo. The left column, advancing towards La Viñuela, was mistakenly attacked by the Ro.37bis who thought they were in the presence of Republican troops. After dropping the first bombs, the airmen realized their mistake when they recognized the silhouette of the Fiat 618.

On Monday, February 8, at 8 a.m., after some skirmishes with the Republicans on the outskirts of the city, the right column entered Malaga. The central column entered at the same time, having sent detachments to occupy the Post and Telegraph building, the Bank of Spain building and the City Hall since 6 a.m. The Duke of Seville's troops entered Malaga around noon. In the port, the Republican fleet sank the gunboats Xauen and Ártabro. The left column, delayed by the destruction of a bridge over the river Alcancin, occupied Vélez-Malaga around 4 pm. At 5 p.m. Gen. Rossi took possession of civil and military powers in Malaga and attended the parade of Italian and Spanish troops.

In the early afternoon of February 8, Roatta ordered the formation of a motorized column to take advantage of his success in Malaga and march to Torre del Mar to join the left column, to which he assigned a reserve bander as reinforcement. The Republicans were then on the run along the coastal road toward Motril. But since no objective other than the capture of Malaga and Vélez-Malaga had initially been set, the formation of the motorized column took time. Commanded by Col. Salvi, it comprised 3 bands (Falco, Indomito and Folgore), the 1st assault tank corps, the 1st m.m. corps, the II gr. 100/17 howitzers, a section of 47/32 guns and a platoon of sappers. The column did not depart

▲ CV 35 at the gates of Malaga on February 7, 1937. (Photo credit: Italian War History Museum)

▲ Howitzer 100/17 mod.14 of the II Gr. on a position overlooking Malaga. (Photo credits: Aymeric Lopez collection)

▼ The gunboat Canovas de Castillo that took part in the bombardments in support of the Nationalist forces advancing along the coastal road. (Photo credit: Juan Antonio Padron Albornoz collection on Vida Maritima)

until the night of 8-9 February at about 1:30 a.m. and reached Torre del Mar at dawn on 9 February. Joining the left column and passing under the command of Colonel Guassardo, the motorized column resumed its advance eastward along the coastal road until it stopped in front of Almuñécar around 10 p.m.

At dawn on February 10, the Guassardo column occupied Almuñécar and headed for Motril. The Republican defense there was particularly effective, helped by the presence of the Guadalpece River, which the Italians had to ford. They lost two L3 pursuers on this occasion. Two Tupolev SB-2s on a bombing mission in the area were attacked by 4 CR.32s of the 5th Sq. One of the bombers was damaged and had to make a crash landing near Motril, in Salobreña. The plane was recovered by the Nationalists, while the crew managed to reach the Republican lines. Around 5 p.m., the CC.NN. took Motril, ending a two-day pursuit over a distance of 119 km. The arrival of the 6th brigada mixta and the 13th brigada internacional in Albuñol stabilized the republican front.

At dawn on February 11, two Tupolev SB-2 bombed the airfield of Granada-Armilla, without success. In the morning, the CR.32 bis of s.Lt. Mantelli and Monti, Sgt. Maj. Drigani and Sgt. Cova of the 4th Sq. intercepted Potez 540 'B' and Potez 542 'Ñ' of the escuadrilla Malraux based in Tabernas, 31 km north of Almeria, returning from a raid on Motril. Their escort of 5 I-15 flew quite far and the Italians took advantage of this, Mantelli shot down the Potez piloted by Guy Santés which crashed into the sea in front of Cabo Sacratif. Mantelli's CR.32 was hit by machine gunner René Deverts and was forced to land in Republican territory, not far from Motril. He was able to return to the Nationalist lines thanks to the help of a peasant. The second Potez was damaged and had to land near Dalías, in Republican territory. The damage was such that it was considered destroyed. This episode led to the dissolution of the Malraux escuadrilla due to the lack of aircraft.

At the same time, communication routes in Republican territory were attacked by the S.81, which targeted the Guadix railway station, as well as the port and the railway station of Almería.

On February 13, Motril was bombed by SB-2s, killing 15 Italian soldiers and wounding 25 others. On the same day, Italian troops left Motril and went up towards Granada. They were relieved by the nationalists.

▲ Italian legionnaires and Lancia 1ZM enter Malaga on February 8, 1937. (Photo credits: Italian Historical Museum of War)

▲▼ Italian troops in the streets of Malaga. (Photo credits: Museo Storico Italiano della Guerra)

▲ Italian legionnaires and Lancia 1ZM in the courtyard of the Malaga town hall. (Photo credits: Archivo ABC)

▼ Franco's troops march along Calle Larios in Malaga.

▲ ▼ Lancia 1ZM in the plaza de la marina of Malaga after the capture of the city by the Nationalists.

▲ The Republican gunboat Xauen that was sunk when Franco's troops arrived in Malaga.
▼ Self-propelled gun of the FAI deactivated by naval artillery in the vicinity of Malaga and captured by the Nationalists on February 8. (Photo credits: Bundesarchiv)

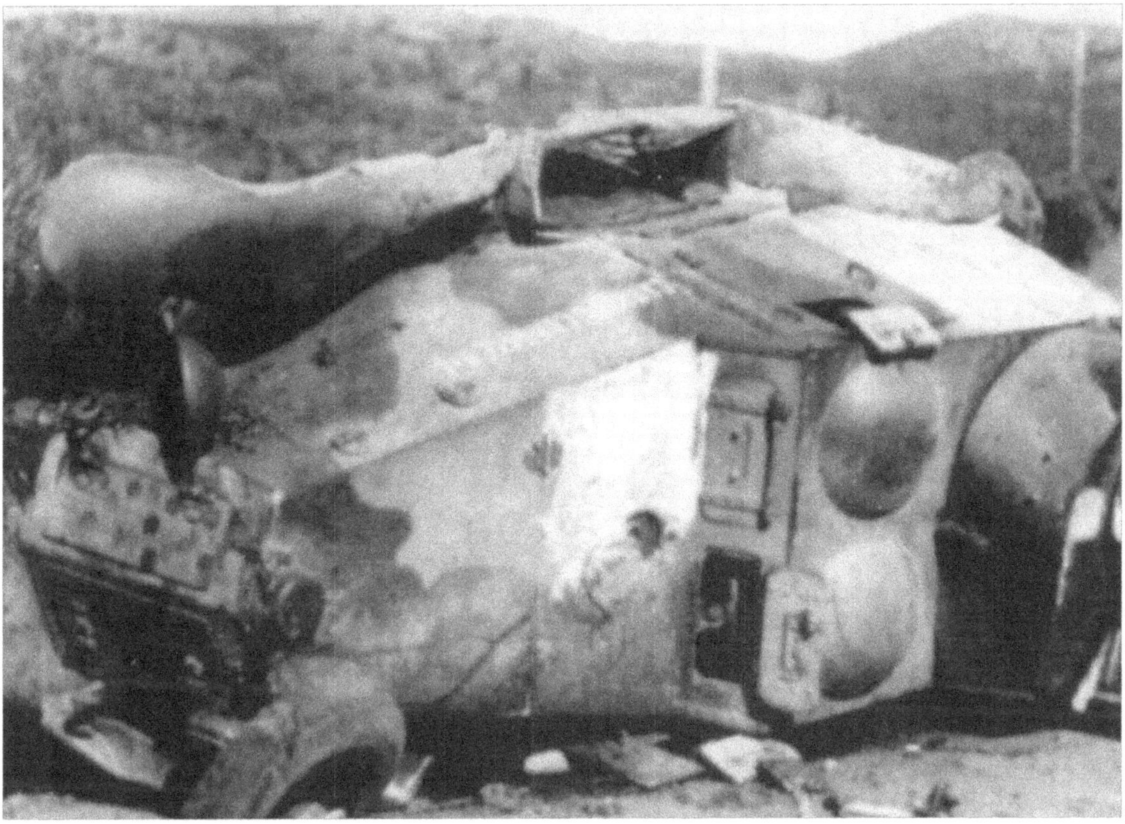

▲ The same self-propelled cannon of the previous page

▼ Potez 540 'B' of the escuadrilla Malraux at Tabernas in early February 1937. (Photo credit: Patrick Laureau collection)

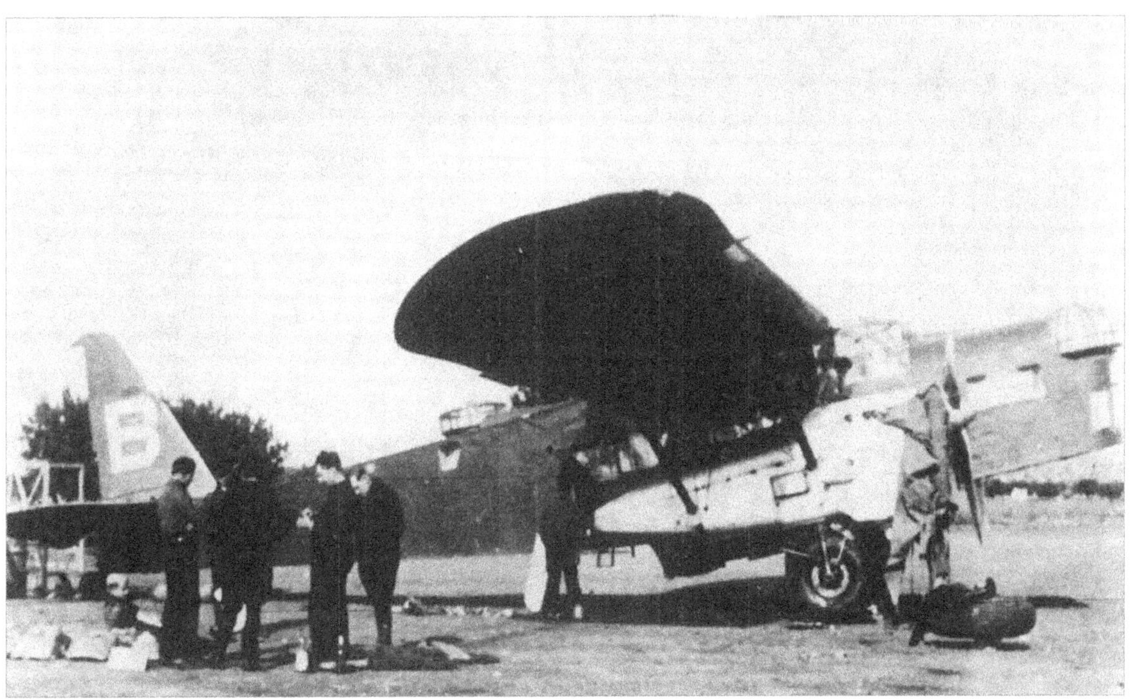

▲ Fiat CR.32 at the airport of Malaga in February 1937. (Photo credits: Dequal family)

▲ ▼ The Tupolev SB-2 hit by CR.32 of the 5th Sq. after its forced landing in Salobreña on February 10, 1937.

▲ Potez 542 'Ñ' of the escuadrilla Malraux in flight.

▼ Pilots of the 4th sq. on the field of Grenada-Armilla in February 1937. (Photo credits: Dequal family)

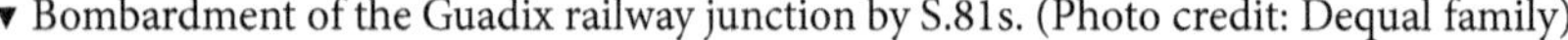

▲ Potez 540 shot down over Cabo Sacratif on February 11, 1937. (Photo credits: Dequal family)
▼ Bombardment of the Guadix railway junction by S.81s. (Photo credit: Dequal family)

RESULTS AND CONSIDERATIONS

The capture of Malaga was a great strategic success for the Nationalist camp, and more specifically for the Italian troops on which the operation depended. In six days of fighting, the Italians lost about 500 men, including about a hundred dead. In the Republican camp, losses were estimated at several hundred dead. Despite the weak armament available to the Republicans, the Battle of Malaga was anything but a simple military march for the Italians. As long as their resistance positions were broken, the Republican fighters showed determined resistance, despite their lack of organization. Colonel Villalba's decision to evacuate Malaga on the evening of February 6, and the fact that he himself abandoned the city, cut off any desire for resistance by the Republican soldiers and militiamen. About 10,000 were captured.

The importance of the capture of Malaga was fundamental from a political point of view: at a time when Franco's troops were blocked in front of Madrid and the morale of the population in Nationalist territory was at its lowest since the beginning of the insurrection, this victory gave them hope for the outcome of the conflict. From a strategic point of view, it gave them access to a large port in the Mediterranean, of which they had been deprived until then, and reduced the length of the front that Queipo de Llano's troops had to hold from 400 to 60 km. For this victory, Roatta received congratulations from Mussolini, Ciano, Queipo de Llano, General José Millan Astray, commander of the Nationalist fleet, and the commander of the Condor Legion. Only Franco remained silent, embarrassed by the fact that the only victory of the Nationalist camp at that time was obtained by foreign forces.

In the Republican camp, General José Asensio Torrado, Undersecretary of War, was dismissed and Colonel Villalba imprisoned. Serving as a true scapegoat, he was released and rehabilitated after more than a year of imprisonment. The real causes of the defeat were the total lack of support from the Valencian government, the lack of discipline within the militia, the struggles between the different factions, the neglect of defense work and the lack of weapons and ammunition. The defeat of Malaga also accentuated tensions between Largo Caballero and the communists, the latter deploring the indulgence of the head of government towards the anarcho-syndicalist militias and his slowness in enforcing conscription.

The tragic events that followed the capture of the Malaga salient were attributed to the Burgos government. None of the Republicans taken prisoner by the Italians were killed, according to the very clear orders issued by Roatta in this regard. Thus, until Gen. Rossi handed over the military and civil powers to Colonel Francisco Borbón y de la Torre, all the Republican prisoners were saved. But soon after the Nationalists took power, a terrible manhunt began even before a court-martial was instituted. Until the end of the war, between 2,250 and 4,235 people were murdered by the Nationalists in retaliation for the 2,500 deaths recorded in Malaga in the first months of the civil war, churches destroyed and aristocratic homes looted.

As for the alleged massacre of the column of refugees fleeing Malaga along the coastal road to Almería, reported by Canadian doctor Norman Bethune, a member of the medical service of the international brigades, there is no Republican document from the time that proves it.

▲ Republican prisoners escorted by Italian legionaries in the Malaga sector. (Photo credit: Museo Storico Italiano della Guerra)

▼ Refugees on the coastal road between Málaga and Almería. (Photo credits: Legado Temboury collection)

BIBLIOGRAPHY

- *La partecipazione italiana alla Guerra Civile Spagnola (1936-1939), Volume I, Testo*, Alberto Rovighi & Filippo Stefani, Stato Maggiore dell'Esercito, Ufficio Storico, 1992

- *La partecipazione italiana alla Guerra Civile Spagnola (1936-1939), Volume I, Documenti e allegati*, Alberto Rovighi & Filippo Stefani, Stato Maggiore dell'Esercito, Ufficio Storico, 1992

- *La guerre d'Espagne, Révolution et contre-révolution (1934-1939)*, Burnett Bolloten, Agone, 2014

- *La guerre d'Espagne*, Anthony Beevor, Calmann-Lévy, 2006 *Les brigades internationales de Franco*, Sylvain Roussillon, Via Romana, 2012

- *Les brigades internationales de Franco*, Sylvain Roussillon, Via Romana, 2012

- *Grandes batallas de la Guerra Civil Española*, Pablo Sagarra, Óscar González, Lucas Molina, La esfera de los libros, 2012

- *Batallas de la Guerra Civil Española*, Lucas Molina Franco, Rafael Permuy López, Fernando Calvo González-Regueral & Juan Vázquez García, Susaeta, 2012

- *Armas y uniformes de la guerra civil española*, Lucas Molina Franco & José María Manrique García, Susaeta, 2009

- *Guerra civil española, Fotografia inéditas*, Isabel Ortiz, Susaeta, 2009

- *Los medios blindados en la Guerra Civil Española, Teatros de operaciones de Andalucía y Centro 36/39*, Artemio Mortera Pérez, Alcañiz Fresno's Editores, 2009

- *Frecce Nere! Le camicie nere in Spagna 1936-1939*, Pierluigi Romeo di Colloredo, Soldiershop-Italia Storica, 2016

- *Guadalajara 1937 la disfatta che non ci fu*, Pierluigi Romeo di Colloredo, Soldiershop-Italia Storica, 2017

- *L'aviazione legionaria in Spagna su due volumi*, Guido Mattioli, Soldiershop-Italia Storica, 2018

- *«In Spagna per l'idea fascista», legionari trentini nella guerra civile spagnola 1936-1939*, Gabriele Ranzato, Camillo Zadra & Davide Znedri, Museo Storico Italiano della Guerra, 2008

- *I volontari stranieri e le brigate internazionali in Spagna (1936-39)*, Bruno Mugnai, Soldiershop Publishing, 2014

- *Guerra di Spagna e aviazione italiana*, Ferdinando Pedriali, Aeronautica Militare Italiana, Ufficio Storico, 1992

- *Ali in Spagna, Immagini e storia della guerra civile 1936-39*, A. Emiliani & G.F. Ghergo, Giorgio Apsotolo Editore, 1997

- *Ali di guerra sulla Spagna, 1936-1939*, Ferdinando Pedriali, IBN Editore, 2015

- *Crickets against Rats, Regia Aeronautica in the Spanish Civil War 1936-1937, Vol.I*, Marek Sobski, Kagero, 2014

- *Aviación en la guerra civil española*, Rafael A. Permuy López, Susaeta, 2012

- *L'impegno navale italiano durante la Guerra Civile Spagnola (1936-1939)*, Franco Bargoni, Ufficio Storico della Marina Militare, 1992

- *Armas y uniformes de la guerra civil española*, Lucas Molina Franco & José María Manrique García, Susaeta, 2009

- *Spanish civil war tanks, The proving ground for blitzkrieg*, Steven J. Zaloga, Osprey Publishing, 2010

- *Blindados italianos en el ejército de Franco (1936-1939)*, Lucas Molina Franco & José María Manrique García, Galland Books, 2009

- *Idrovolanti italiani nei cieli iberici, Una rassegna dei velivoli forniti alla Spagna tra il 1922 e il 1938 e in servizio nell'Aeronáutica Naval*, Tullio Marcon & Angelo Emiliani, Aerofan n°93, 2005

- *L'aviación de el Tercio*, Paolo Waldis, Storia Militare n°240, 2013

- *«In Spagna per l'idea fascista», legionari trentini nella guerra civile spagnola 1936-1939*, Gabriele Ranzato, Camillo Zadra & Davide Znedri, Museo Storico Italiano della Guerra, 2008

- *I volontari stranieri e le brigate internazionali in Spagna (1936-39)*, Bruno Mugnai, Soldiershop Publishing, 2014

- *Air War over Spain, Aviators, Aircraft and Air Units of the Nationalist and Republican Air Forces 1936-1939*, Rafael A. Permuy López, Ian Allan Publishing, 2009

- *Soviet Merchant Marine. Civil War in Spain 1936-1939* (shipsnostalgia.com)

▲ Captain Vincenzo Dequal (Paride Limonesi)

TITOLI GIÀ PUBBLICATI - TITLES ALREADY PUBLISHING

BOOKS TO COLLECT